HOW ROBOTS IMPROVE ORGANIZATIONAL PERFORMANCE

JOHN LOK

2018 Nov Seven Print Published

Contents

Preface

Introduction

This book divides two part : Artificial intelligence raises productive efficiency and service performance. This book part first is concerned how to apply artificial intelligent machine or robot to raise productivive efficiency in factory.Research question: How to apply artificial intelligence to raise labor productive efficiency? Research question: How to apply (AI) technology to raise labor efficiencies or productivities?

The first part is intended to explain why and how (AI) technology and raising productivity or efficiency has close relationship. First part gives some artificial intelligence technologic concepts to indicate why and how (AI) can raise labor productive efficiency to assist labor to work in factories. This book first part is suitable to any managers have interest to learn how to apply (AI) technological productive method to achieve economic benefit in factories . In this part, the main important aim, I give examples to explain how to apply (AI) technology to raise labor productive efficiencies really.

Research question: How to apply (AI) technology to assist employees to improve service performance to serve clients?

This book second part is concerned how to apply (AI) technology to raise service performance. Also I shall compare to explain what advantages and disadvantages when the organization either choose to apply (AI) or not choose (AI) to assist employees to serve clients, these any one sample industry encounters customer complains, due to it lacks (AI) technologic assistance to aim to let any reader to judge whether how to choose the solvable method is better. In, conclusion, this book can provide sample industries to let students to feel whether (AI) technology will raise labor productivities or efficiency or service performance.

In part two, it shall indicate how the process of (AI) technologic robots field develops to assist employees to serve clients to let they feel more satisfactory and reduce any unreasonable complains. I shall indicate underground train and Disney entertainment theme park and University and unground train transportation and environmental protection businessmen etc. enterprises to explain how which can apply (AI) robotic machines to assist employees to provide more excellent service to let them to feel.

Thus, I shall assume that if one company or individual businessman can apply (AI) technology to assist employees to serve clients in shopping center or restaurant etc. or assist them to produce any products in factories. Then they have more confidence to attract more clients or reduce labour turnover. I shall give insurance and travel both industries to explain how to apply (AI) technology to serve insurance or travelling clients solve consumer behavioral prediction as well as I shall indicate some methods to explain how to apply (AI) technology to assist manufacturers or service providers to attempt to solve some challenges encountering when who attempt to raise service performance or productive efficiencies.

Nowadays, artificial intelligent robotic technology which is one kind of popular tool to help workers to work in factories or offices or serve clients in restaurants or shopping centers. It brings this question: Can artificial intelligent robotic machine men assist workers to raise productive efficiencies or improve service performance?

If one factory or one office only applies artificial intelligent robotic machine men to replace human labors to help its different departments to do any tasks, whether can its (AI) robotic machine men help them to raise productive efficiencies ? If one restaurant or one shopping center only apply (AI) robotic machine men to help to serve clients, whether can its (AI) robotic machine men help them to improve service performance? Is it better to apply half manual labors and half (AI) robotic machine men to work in one organization in order to raise productive efficiencies or improve

service performance?
In my this book, I shall indicate some cases to explain how and why (AI) robotic machine men can either raise productive efficiencies or improve service performance or they can't either raise productive efficiencies or improve service performance in any situations. Managers or employees can evaluate whether how to apply (AI) robotic machine men to assist them to work in their workplaces in order to achieve the most beneficial advantages to their organization's different departments' raising productivity and efficiency and service performance improvement aims.

Prologue

BRIEF CONTENTS

Why social behavior may influence organizational strategy needs to be changed ?
How and why human behavior may influence economic growth or recession? p.61-95

ONE

(AI) TECHNOLOGY CAN RAISE LABOR EFFORT STRATEGY

What is the relationship between (AI) robotic service behavior and improving service performance behavior

In what way has globalization affected employers choose online work to provide to local or overseas to raise productivity? Is online work still a useful working place environment for local and overseas employers to raise productivity in a globalized online age, such as online electronic books' authors, online office administration or online surveys or online researchers etc. kind of online jobs supplying? Our age is entering an online business environment, such as online electronic air tickets sale, online electronic books publishing, online advertising and online shopping and website design service promotion , online university education etc. different kind of online businesses from internet. It seems online channel can increase global online job chances to affect that our live and our job nature to be changed every day. For example, online electronic book publishing business will be popular, many different countries' readers who like to buy electronic books to study, due to these online electronic book shops, e.g. Amazon, lulu, book Rix, book tango etc. electronic book stores which can provide free charge to deliver cheaper paper books to any overseas countries' readers' homes and which paper book prices are more cheaper to compare to book shops' paper books process after who have paid to buy any electronic books or paper books from these online book stores websites. Moreover, these readers can read these book stores' electronic books from online publishing sellers' websites to download these electronic books to study at homes or any libraries etc. computer provision of places easily and conveniently. So readers do not need to walk to any book shops to buy any paper books and who also do not need to bring any heavy paper books back to homes conveniently. Hence, electronic publishers can provide electronic book authors' job chances to write their books and type to computers to register to be online authors to publish whose electronic or paper books to earn loyalty income at home very easily. Also, the globalizing online job nature can change the customized office work style. It won't need staffs go to office to work from 9:00 AM to 6:00 PM. In general office workers need to spend eight to ten working hours with five or six working days within per week commonly. Hence, online office workers don't need to pay transportation fee and lunch cost, due who can work at their home when who turn on their computer to enter whose employers' websites to work and make email communication to connect between them conveniently. So, I feel the online electronic book authors and online office administration jobs which will be popular further occupations to be provided from global online job structure style and many labors will like to work online, then who can raise productivity conveniently when who work at home in the future. Beside, due to online (internet) is very popular and cheap cost to be needed to spend expenditure from employer. So, internet will build the relationships between workplaces and every staff role identity and everyday life and online working environments can connect them to work in the process of globalization in the future. Also, our everyday life and work is entering in a globalizing world. It emphasizes on time and space compression and the importance of virtual space and experience in our daily lives of many people, the working style seems spent online working time to change how our social traditional work roles and our traditional office working places-based environments to home online working environments further long time in the future. So, employers ought plan to prepare online working methods to let their employees to raise productivity. IN the future, it is possible that (AI) technology can be applied to online computer channel to assist any human computer workers to raise their efficiency and productivity on computer industry, e.g. programmer, computer technician, website creator. etc. different kinds of computer related occupations. So, programmers can have more program creating effort when they can be assisted by (AI) clever mind effort influence or website creator can be given ideas how to create website to raise more attraction to let website clients to have more attractive website choice to buy their website design service. Hence, future (AI) robotic technology can have more creative effort to assist computer occupation workers to raise more creative effort.

Why will (AI) technologic knowledgeable robotic workers be raised productivity ?

Future, (AI) robotic workers can assist knowledge labors to raise productivity from internet channel. Social science can explain knowledgeable jobs will be useful and popular and assisting labors to raise productivity to work at home online working environments. Within social science, in such discipline is sociology and human psychology and geography which indicates internet technology have changed to online working place environment, sense of working place, online employee role identity, everyday online work and life style, website global working communication and email online communication working interconnections. It seems internet brings access to social, economic and political resources to effect change to both individual and social working conditions, such as employers accept to attempt to use internet to assist office staffs to work at home, e.g. many book publishing businesses like to attempt to publish electronic books from online book store, instead of book shops channel to sell paper books. So these online book stores give chance to authors to publish electronic books or online paper books from online sale channel to earn loyalty income. For example, Amazon online electronic bookstore can publish electronic books and online paper books to sell all one day 24 hours to any countries' readers from its website, so when any countries' readers can enter its website to choose any different kind of subjects of electronic books to buy by visa card conveniently. Such as fiction, psychology, economy, science, law, architecture, medicine, commerce, management etc. subjects. So, any country's reader who does not need to buy air tickets to go to the country's book shop to buy the paper book, who only needs to pay visa card to buy the electronic or online paper books from Amazon publishing's website to buy any countries' electronic and paper books and then the overseas reader can choose either to download it from whose home computer or pays more price to deliver the online paper book to post to whose country conveniently. Hence, this online bookstore sale method will be popular and many free work authors will choose to work to raise the productivity of more quality electronic books numbers from this internet channel.

However, the consequences of global change are far from uniform with globalizing influences and adapted as new technological, economic and online working cultural experiences are incorporated by any countries' staffs of any cities, towns and rural areas into their everyday work lives from long distance easily. Since one company can employ different countries' staffs to work from internet working channel at their homes. For example, a America company can employ overseas countries' staffs to work at the same time together by sending job duties from email communication channel among them when the America company has any job arrangement to notify to any staff to finish it any time, then the overseas staff finish the job and who can send whose finished documents to whose America employer any time. It seems the overseas staffs whose working hours can be flexible and those working hours have no regular office working hours to be fixed time table, so they do not need to work in any fixed working time table every working days, who can send their finished office documents to whose employers after who have finished their documents by either email communication channel or office online website downloads office download any time conveniently.

It will be a new working style position that online working globalization is in a new stage. We are living in an age of very rapid and fluid flow of information, ideas, products and people which are having an effect of a variety of scales. I shall indicate evidences to explain why employers will encounter online knowledgeable jobs to raise productivity in a globalizing world by sociology concept. I shall focus on research into the connections between our everyday online life style, online working place and online working role identity. The first is that everyday online life is the manifestation of social existence and always involves either distant or direct interaction with other people. Such as we can use internet email channel to communicate with overseas friends or strange people, even employers or employees can also use email to exchange to receive and send their office documents by email or company website any time conveniently. Good example includes such things are as online participation in work, employment, cultural events, and recreation, shopping and communication from internet channel. It is related to employees are working in whose home working places and their home working place are possible to connect their overseas employers' offices and however, readily these may be separated in far distant conceptual terms, such as an online working environment. The employee's home is such whose employer's office, who can work at home from online channel conveniently. When who receives whose employer's email about what job duties who needs to do every day. Then, who sees his employer's email, then either if who did not understand how to do whose job duties clearly, who can send email back to ask whose employers to explain how who needs to do whose office job duties by email communication channel again easily. Even after who finish whose office job duties on that day or another day, then who can send finished office job duties to whose employers by email conveniently. In this view, online working places and sense of online working places are produced by different countries' large enterprise employers and overseas employees interacting together. At the same time, employees and employers whose sense are contacted by employees' individual role identity from email or office website communication channel any time. Thus, traditional office working environment is constrained and enabled by different countries' working histories and cultures and social class backgrounds and economic conditions and job opportunities, working positions of power and working geographical locations and development of local change and distant social interaction. In the future, online working place will be changed from traditional socially significant to online social relationship; underlying this sense of online working place will be the notion that some employers and employees themselves ought feel that life. Moreover, online working place is the possibility of non controlling employees' working time, due to working hours are flexible and employers' working places sizes are very limited to supply to many staffs to work in a limited office working place in the same working time. It seems online home environment will be very popular, due to every employee will use whose home to work to finish whose office documents at home every day any time very conveniently as well as employers won't need to spend much expenditure to pay for large sizes of office rent when the employer needs to rent more than one room office at more than one floor in one building. Hence, company's website expenditure can reduce the employers' office rent seriously. Moreover, employees can be dominated by feelings towards changing general office working place to online working at home as well as changing fixed working time table to flexible working time table, e.g. the staff can see whose employer's email to know what office job duties who needs to do tonight, so who will finish whose office documents and will send whose finished office documents to whose employer by email tomorrow. So, home online working environment is seen as an ideal home working place, and home online working environment which is quiet, safe and it has certain valued facilities and home online working environment is such as the type of residents in the employee's living building. This sense of living and online work place will be held by residents who will be employed in professional/ managerial/ technical etc. occupations. Hence, local employees won't catch any transportation to go to office as well as overseas employees won't also catch planes to go to whose employer's country's office to work, due to who can use online email communication or office website communication channels to work together conveniently. However, working facilities will be one online computer working commodity which is purchasable, useable and exchangeable and saleable to any employees are located at home and employers are located at office, and after a flexible working time table is discarded easily by employer, due to whose website or office email can receive any employee's individual finished office documents by every employee's individual email communication any time very conveniently. Moreover, home online working place is also like a stage on every employee's life is lived out. The employee will feel that whose life and working time is lived at home together at the same time. Similar to feel commodity sense of home and the working place which are the same location, but it is distinguished from it by the establishment of arriving strange and far distant of the employee's local or overseas employer's office when the employee's working place is family interacting to the employee's house or home.

Our world is entering globalization, people are connecting in an increasing number of ways. It is clear also that is the face of globalization, the ways of our everyday working life is either constituted which are still shaped by local expenditure of working place or is by where the firm's overseas employees love locally, regionally and nationally or is by the access who have limited to office resources and home office online working locations opportunity changing from general office working environment to home online working environment. Roberston (1992) shows is that" this is not just about economic processes, but about social and cultural issues are as well. In the early part of the 21 ST century, it is necessary to see this as a set of processes that encompass economic, political, social, cultural and environmental changes."

Why does (AI) technologic knowledgeable jobs will raise economic benefits to organizations?

Future, (AI) technological jobs will be applied to internet gather (big data gathering technology) to help businessmen to gather competitors' data to predict future consumer behaviors in short time. Is globalization influenced to new online knowledgeable jobs to be provided to raise low income level worker's living od standard? One of the key areas of debate among theorists is the extent to which globalization is a new phenomenon or stage in a process. When it began and the path that it has followed and thus how new it is. Such as internet is used in communication aspect in early, e.g. hospital or war email communication channel. Then, many businessmen discovered online electronic commerce is also one online sale and purchase method. So, it will cause online office workers or online freelance online jobs, e.g. electronic book authors working style or electronic book reading cultural existed in our society in common possibly in the future. However, I recognize globalization is a misleading concept since what is described as globalization has been happening for the 500 years history ago. Rather what is new is that human are entering an age of transition, such as online knowledgeable workers or knowledgeable nature of different jobs will be caused from online working environment popularly.

There are key processes of globalization: the economic, often is seen as the central process, the political, social, cultural and online working environment. Every natural economy needs to maintain the rate of growth, employment, welfare provision and minimum wage balance levels, so it will cause knowledgeable jobs provided, such as online organized labors, it also will change the traditional office organizational environment to cause online new organizational home work environment popularly in the future. Hence, economic and political has close connection, political and cultural has also close connection, cultural and social has also close connection, social and working environment has also connection. After all these connections cause globalization finally, then the new online knowledgeable working environment, such as online jobs will be required by global office employees popularly in the future. It will bring many online workers supply to the employment market in the future. As capital in the new globalized economy has a limited attachment to working place, production centers, such as offices, factories or farms which locate any where it is competitively advantages to do so, and economic activity moves to where labor is cheapest or raw materials is the least expensive. It can be raised demand to online knowledgeable workers demand in global competitive employment environment directly. For example, cultural, social, global expansion of Mc Donald's and other fast food chains will be entered to the online sale channel from (AI) technologic assistance. Hence, environmental globalization raises human awareness, includes a new view of the natural and the social worlds to environmental protection message. These message source is from online channel popularly nowadays. Online organizing environment and living will influence our everyday working worlds. Due to many industrial cities and life will be not needed by global employers. However, industrial cities concentrate on demanding in developing countries, e.g. China, India, Korea etc. countries. So, developed countries, such as America, England, Japan etc. countries' employers will need many online knowledgeable employees to help them to work from online work place environment popular in the future. Later, knowledgeable online working environment will be popular to developing countries when which economy had developed mature in the future. So, it is possible online jobs will raise low income level householders' living of standard when (AI) robotic technology is applied to internet technology.

What benefits will bring when (AI) robotic technology is applied to internet technology:

Productivity growth can reduce production costs and increase returns on investments. Some of which provide greater income for business owners which some are given higher wages to labours. However, the productivity of individuals may be reflected in employment rates, wage rates, stability of employment, job satisfaction or employability across jobs or industries. The productivity of enterprises, in addition to output per worker may measure in terms of market share and export performance. The benefits to societies from higher individual and enterprise productivity may be evident in increased competitiveness and employment or in a shift of employment from low to higher productivity sector. So, employers can use this method to measure every employee's morality and job behaviour performance to judge whether their job ethic and job attitude whether which can adopt to continue to work in whose organizational environment. If the employer discovered the employee's morality and job behaviour performance and job attitude is not achieved to whose work performance standard, then who can decide to either reduce whose salary or dismiss him/her or not increasing whose salary for long term any decision. So, labour ethic issue is very important to influence economic growth to any countries.

Whether labour ethic has close relationship to economic growth. I feel this issues concerns any stage of the labour life cycle and organization life cycles, it includes the link between the design of economic theory and labour individual morality and job behaviour and performance. In fact, we need to suppose all research questions and labour economy is as mapping to particular stages of an individual's life cycle to labour economy ought be related to the accumulation of human (labour) capital, labour market entry and labour supply choices, behaviour within firms and household decision making. Prior years some researchers had been carrying on observing experiments to the women and men labour work and in whose nature environment for weeks, and then used various treatments, including manipulating the environment in such a way to increase and decrease rest periods. They got result long time working hours and not rest time, it will reduce labours(workers) of productivity. So, it implies the overall productivity and individual productivity will be reduced. Although, the employers have enough workers to work in the natural working environment at the same time, but due to who have no enough rest time to provide to them, then their workers' working performance and efficiency will be fallen. Nowadays, industrialized countries had began to consider how to plan similar welfare reforms, researching the economic reasons and consequences to labour economic issue, such as United States, the United King, Sweden and Germany, it seems economic growth and law ethic has close relationship. However, labour economy includes how to measure labour's emotion to raise productivity, as well as how technological change, education, employment and wages which can assist labour to raise productivity. Due to good labour emotion and labour ethic can raise productivity, then raising productivity can also raise economic growth finally. So, I believe which have close cause and effect relationship.

However, many economists have long been pessimistic that an experimental approach could offer such illustrations of labour ethic and economic growth of cause and effect relationship in their field. Who feel labour bad emotion or bad labour ethic has no any influence to economic growth. In fact, the economic world is extremely complicated, so human needs to have economic laws is set by controlled experiment to measure or judge whether labour ethic and economic growth which has or has no any close relationship. If economists have no such test, economic laws, who can't perform such as the controlled experiments of chemists or biologists very well because who can't easily control other important factors to observe why labour emotion or ethic has reason to influence overall economic growth to any country if they neglect to carry on researching experiment between the relationship of ethic and productivity and economic growth. So I recommend economists need have participants in the natural field experiment to carry on researching to any labour emotion or ethic issue to gather statistic information of population to get prediction more accurately if who want to measure whether labour emotion or ethic and productivity which has close relationship to any country's economic growth for long term.

TWO

(AI) TECHNOLOGY CAN RAISE EMPLOYEE SERVICE PERFORMANCE

What is the relationship between (AI) robotic service behavior and improving service performance behavior

How and why (AI) technology can be applied to service industry? I shall explain how (AI) technology can encourage consumption behaviors when it is applied to service industry as below. I shall apply behavioral economic theory to (AI) technology to indiate how it can enourage consumption when it is applied to service industry.

At the core of behavioral economics is used psychology of economics analysis to improve economics on its own terms generating theoretical insights, making better prediction of field consumption of behavioral phenomena, and suggesting better policy to any company or government decision makers. It rejects economic theories based on utility maximization, equilibrium and efficiency. It is useful because it provides economists with a theoretical framework that can be applied to almost any form of economic (and even non-economic) behavior to predict behavioral consumption more easily to businessmen. So, behavioral economy is different to general economy concept, it applies psychological methods to attempt to predict consumption behavior.

Simpifying much assumption that are not central to the economic theory to apply to psychological behavior. Other assumption simply acknowledge human limits on computational power and self-interest. These assumptions can be considered procedurally rational because human needs to solve problems that are often so complex that who can't be solved exactly by even modern computer technology. So, if businessmen apply psychological method to predict behavioral consumption to earn the more benefits or profit, it is more reasonable to compare to apply computer methods to predict consumption behavior.

Theories in behavioral economics should be judged by reality, generality and tractability concepts to apply why we (consumers) do our behavior (consumption of choices) from psychological analysis. We share the positivist view that the ultimate test of a theory is the accuracy of its predictions. But we also believe that better predictions are likely to result from theories with more realistic assumptions. In psychology, such as connectionist models that capture some of the essential features of neural functioning, which are based on utility maximization, yet are reaching the point where they are able to predict many judgemental and behavioral phenomena. Contrary to the positivistic view, however, businessmen ought believe that predictions of consumers' feelings (e.g., of subjective well-being) should be an important goal to earn more profit more easily.

Most of the ideas in behavioral economics are not new. When economics first became identified as a distinct field of study, psychology didn't exist as a discipline to apply to economy subject.

For example, "invisible hand" and "the wealth of Nations" which belong to theory to moral sentiments, which laid out psychological principles of individual behavior that are arguably as profound as whose economic observations. Another example, such as a simple model of social utility means that one (consumer) or person's utility was affected by another person's , such as whose family or friends' influence why to choose to buy this product or use this service in consumption market.

Nowadays, economists hoped their discipline could be like a natural science to apply psychological methods to predict behavioral consumption to assist businessmen to earn more economic benefit or to reduce cost or profit to win whose competitors. But psychology was not very scientific. However, later economists are very much appealed to psychological insights to attempt to assist businessmen how to predict consumers how who will prefer to choose to consume to buy this product or use this service.

Throughout the second half of the century, many criticisms of the positivistic perspective took place in both economics and psychology. The economists of the time had less disagreement with psychology than they realized. They assume without foundation that behavior always aims at the goal of maximum pleasure and minimum pain; but behavior is not goal-oriented. Also the economists of the time believed false conclusions are drawn from false psychological assumptions to predict consumer individual behavioral consumption wrongly.

The importance of psychological measures and bounds on rationality. These commentators attracted attention, but did not alter the fundamental direction of economics. One development was the rapid acceptance by economists of the expected utility and discounted utility models which are making decision under uncertainty and choice, respectively. Whereas the assumptions and implications of utility analysis are rather flexible, and the expected utility and discounted utility models have numerous precise and testable implications. So, it seems economy and psychology can have close relationship to be connect to be applied to predict consumer individual consumption of behavior to assist any enterprises can earn more profit or more economic benefit more easily in global competitive consumption market nowadays.

In behavioral economy view, economists began to accept counter examples that could be not be permanently ignored, developments in psychology identified promising directions for new theory to be applied how to assist businessmen to predict behavioral consumption to earn economic benefits or profits. Beginning around 1960 year, psychology became to be dominated by the brain as an information-processing device replacing the behaviorist conception of the brain as a stimulus-response machine. The information-processing permitted a fresh study of neglected topics like memory, problem solving and decision making. These new topics were more obviously relevant to the conception of utility maximization than behaviorism had appeared to be to apply how to predict behavioral consumption in traditional psychological method.

However, behavioral economy and psychological consumption prediction method, psychologists began to use economic models as a benchmark against which to constrast their psychological models. Early research in behavioral consumption methds have followed these steps. First, identify assumption or models that are used by economists, who expected utility and discounted utility. Second, the assumption or model is a rule out alternative explanations (such as subjects' confusion or transactions costs). And third, the assumption or model creates alternative theories that generalize existing models. The final is to construct economic models of behavior using the behavioral assumptions to test them from the third step. This final step of economic models of behavior has only been taken more recently to be applied to predict why the consumer prefers to choose to do this behavioral consumption of decision finally. So, (AI) technology is one kind of consumption psychological tool to encourage consumption behavior when it is applied to service industry, due to it can improve staffs' service performance to let clients to feel more satisfactory service to the businessmen.

What is the standard economic model? It is the standard economic model, the way most economists think about consumer welfare and consumer choice. What is the rationality in the standard economic model? The standard economic model relies heavily on the assumption that consumers are rational. Standard economic model assumes that consumers are fully aware of all the options who have, who can always and consistently , rank whose options in accordance with their preferences, and always choose the option, who like the best option. Thus, what the assumptions of the standard economic model of consumer are? The assumptions include consumers act with full information, consumers have known preferences, consumers choose the best option available. In economic view point, It concerns consumers will compare cost to make decision to choose to buy which kind of product which can satisfy whose needs among of similar products of comparision.

The standard economic model of consumer behavioral (AI) robotic service tool advantages includes:

A logically consistent theory of consumer behavior can be built, that theory can be used to make predictions about consumer behavior and those predictions can be compared with reality and those models often correspond to actual behavior of consumption reasons. What is the inconvenient truth? It includes clear evidence from psychology has shown that the rationality assumptions of standard economic model are wrong. Evidence from psychology has shown that consumers often are irrational and also who are predictably irrational. So these are wrong view point to influence how economists judge what cause consumption of behavior. Thus, it beings this question? What is mean of predictably irrational? It means that of irrational consumers were irrational in random ways, who would cancel each other out, leaving the overall outcomes determined by the behavioral consumption of rational consumers. As that case, behavioral economic theories that ignored irrational behavioral consumption would work just fine. But, psychology has shown that consumers are irrational in similar and predictable ways. Therefore, irrationality doesn't cancel out and can't be ignored to judge why the behavioral consumption has been caused.

How can behavioral economists judge each behavioral consumption cause? Economists will see evidence that consumers often are unable to make use of what consumers know about whose available options and whose preferences to figure out the best available option. However, although economic theory doesn't always assume self- interested behavior to any consumers, as a practical matter, most applications of economic theory assume that consumers act according to self- interest to decide every behavioral consumption of choice. For insurance industry is one good behavioral economy market example, insurance market competition can make rational consumption. Such as competitive market in auto vehicle accident insurance will charge very high rates to some insurance buyers who might to drive a fast speed, but unsafe motorbike, this one might argue will protect the driving insurance buyers from taking stupid risk. So learning can make rational consumers. Even if consumers are predictably irrational, who can learn from their families and other consumer' or friends behavioral mistakes, therefore, over time irrational consumers will learn to be rational to make the most irrational consumption. As a result, there are few opportunities to learn from consumer individual mistakes of any consumption of decision. Finally, if there are many potential; bad choices and one good consumption of choice, it might take a lot of costly experimentation to figure out the right consumption of choice. Thus, the standard economic model of behavioral consumption of prediction method, which is standard economic theories assume that consumers are rational, strong-willed , and self-interested, but evidence from psychology shows that who are not and that evidence also shows that consumer individual irrationality has predictable features. So, it seems behavioral economic model can make economic predictions more accurate by using the evidence on consumer individual predictable irrational behavioral prediction in any kind of the similar products in competitive market nowadays.

How to apply (AI) robotic service techology to raise or improve service performance?

The methods to predict how to cause the (consumer's)person's consumption of behavior are the same as those in other areas of economic and psychological methods. In fact, behavioral economics relied heavily on evidence generated to predict behavioral consumption by experiments. More recently, however, behavioral economists have moved beyond experimentation and the full range of methods are employed by economists. The experiements played a large role in the initial phase of behavioral economics because experimental control is exceptionally helpful for distinguishing behavioral explanations from standard ones.

Suppose we observed this phenomenon in these any one of cares, in the form of failures of legal cases to settle before trial, costly divorce proceedings, and labor strikes. They are phenomenons of human' behaviours are caused by costs and benefits measurement of result. It implies the married people or the legal compensatory amount or labor strikes compensatory benefits will evaluate whether thier economic benefit is more or loss is more to decide divorce behavior or legal trial behavior or labour strikes compensatory behavior . So, consumer individual psychological behavior and economic benefits has close relationship to cause how consumer who prefers to make any consumption of choice every day. As the failures of legal cases to settle before trial , the behavioural economy concept would be difficult to tell whether rejection of offers was the result of reputation-building in repeated games, agency problems (between clients and lawyers) confusion why the lawyer' client (appellant) who choose to continue to attempt to pay legal fee to find the lawyer to appellate the case if the case is fail at the first time . However, in these game experiments of failures of legal cases to settle before trial, costly divorce proceedings, and labor strikes. These explanations are ruled out because the experiments are played once, have no agents, and are simple enough to rule out confusion. Thus, the experimental data clearly establish that subjects are expressing concern for fairness.

Other experiments have been useful for testing whether judgment errors which individuals commonly make in psychology experiments also affect prices and quantities in markets, such as shareholder's individual investment behavior. The lab is especially useful for these studies because individual and market-level data can be observed. Although behavioral economists relied on experimental datato predict shareholder's individual investment behavior, however, behavioral economics subject is seen as a very different method from experimental economics. As noted, behavioral economists are methodological profession. They define themselves, not on the basis of the research methods that who employ, but rather their application of psychological insights to economics.

Experimental economists, on the other hand, define themselves on the basis of use of experimentation which is as a research tool. Also, economists have made a major investment in developing experimental methods that are suitable for addressing economic issues, and have achieving among themselves on a number of important issues. For example, experimental economists often make instructions and software available for precise replication, and raw data are typically shared for reanalysis. Experimental economists also insist on paying performance-based. However, experimental economists have also developed rules that many behavioral economists are likely to find excessively . For example, experimental economists rarely collect data like demographics, self-reports, reponse times and other cognitive measure which behavioral economists have found useful. Descriptions of the experimental environment are usually abstract rather than which are carried on experiment in the outside world because economic theory rarely makes a prediction about how a happen would matter, and experimenters are concerned about losing control over incentives if choosing strategies with certain labels is appealing because of the labels themselves. Finally, economic experiments also typically use "stationary replication", in which the same task is repeated over and over in each period. Data from the last few periods of the experiment are typically used to draw conclusions about equilibrium behavior outside the lab. When economists believe that examining behavior after it is of great interest, it is also obvious that many important aspects of economic consumption of individual behavior to every individual consumer. The consumer's individual consumption of behavioral choose is like the first few periods of an experiment rather than the psychological methods to predict behavioral consumption.

Supposing if we need to make decision of marriage, educational decisions, and saving for retirement, or the purchase of large durables like houses, sailboats, can cars, which happen just a few times in a person's life, a focus on behavior is clearly not warranted. All said, the focus on psychological realism and economic applicability of research promoted by the behavioral-economics perspective suggests the usefullness research outside the lab and of a broader range of approaches to laboratory research. So, economists realize that who have ideal opportunity to learn by trial-and-error, in a stationary environment, and uses the opportunity to learn how to carry on experimenting any psychology and behavioral researches in lab experiment environment.

What is psychology of consumption behavior?

Psychology is the science of human behavior and mental consumption processes. In consumption process behavior, it is any consumption behaviors as well as consumer mental consumption process is consumer individual internal experiences, comparison with alternative products, products choice of the best, making decision to consume or not consume for the product. So, advertisers often persuade to influence consumers' behavior to attract them to choose to buy whose products.

Why businessmen need to learn consumer psychology? Because psychology can help businessmen scientifically to evaluate common consumer beliefs and misconceptions about consumption behavior and consumption decision making mental processes. Consumption scientific psychology has four basic goals: To describe , explain, predict and change consumption behavior and consumption decision making mental process. Consumption psychological information is based on evidence, this is information based on direct observation and measurements with consumption behavior with scientific method. How are typical images of psychology? Consumption psychologists need to use scientific method to help businessmen to think what predicts who own, make a list of words would who use to describe a psychological scientist and what use to describe a psychological scientist and what images the businessmen have. However, consumption psychologists have difference ways of looking at the same problem for the businessmen, which is why there are so many sub-fields of consumption psychology. Consumption psychology's roots began in philosophy, but the focus changes to a scientific focus consumer.

Behaviorism is focused on consumer buying behavior that can be measured and observable. This returned the scientific approach to consumption psychology. Consumption behaviorist's believe consumers are controlled by their environment. Consumption behaviorism focuses on consumption observable behavior. However, consumption cognitive psychology believes that consumption behaviors are preformed because of the product ideas and thoughts. The cognitive perspective focuses on such consumer decision making and choice processes, such as perception, memory and thinking to the product.

The two categories of consumer's behavioral consumption of decision

Consumers will choose to use the businessman's service when who can provide (AI) service workers to serve them more than the businessman who can not provide (AI) service workers to serve them. The field of consumer's behavioral consumption of decision research, on which behavioral economics has drawn more than any other subfield of psychology, typically classifies research into two categories: judgement and choice. Judgement research deals with the processes people use to estimate probabilities. Choice deals with the processes people use to select among actions, considering of any relevant judgements who may have made. Everyday, we, such as consumers need to make probable judements. Due to judging the likelihood of events is central to economic life. For example: Will you lose your job in a poor economic environment? Will you be able to find another house you like as much as the one you must bid for right away? Will the government raise interest rates in this year or next year? Will a merger strategy increase profits? These questions are answered by some process of judging likelihood. The standard principles used in economic to model probability judgement in economic are concepts of statistical sampling, which are concerned probabilities in the face of new evidence. However, it requires a separation between previously judged probabilities and evaluations of new evidence. However, (consumers) people often overestimate the probability who previously attached to events which later happened. This leads to "secondguessing". For example, Monday morning quarterbacking and may be partly responsible for lawsuits against stockbrokers who lost money for their clients. (The clients think the brokers should have known). For example, anybody has tried to learn from a computer distance learning manual has seen the classroom learning of knowledge in action. Another example for making probability judgements is called "representativeness": People judge conditional probabilities like P(hypothesis /data) or P(example/class) by how well the data represents the hypothesis or the example represents the class. Representativeness is an economical shortcut that delivers reasonable judgements with minimal effort in many cases. For example, in judging whether a certain student (University customer) described in a profile is, say, a psychology major or computer science major, the student decides how well the profile matches the psychology or computer science career to the student generally. So, University can read the student profile to predict whether the student will choose to study psychology subject more prefer or computer subject more prefer to predict whose computer or psychology student numbers more accurate in the year. So, such as university cause, if the university can apply (AI) technology to predict or evalute whether the student will choose which subject to study, then they can make more accurate subjects arrangement to let students to study more easily.

Reference

Adrian, P. (2012). Introduction to marketing theory & practice, 3 rd edition, London: Oxford press.

Couper, M.P. J. Blair and T. Triplet (1999). A Comparison Of Mail And E-mail For a Survey Of Employees In USA Statistical Agencies. Journal Of Official Statistics, 15, 39-56.

Data monitor (2008). The proctor and gamble company. Retrieved Nov. 15 2009 from http://www.datamonitor.com/

Dyer, D., F. Dalzell & R. Olegario (2004). Rising tide. Lessons learned from 165 years of brand building at Procter and Gamble. Boston, MA: Havard Business School Press.

Priesnitz, W. (2007) Counting Our Food Miles. Natural Life, 1 July.

Sullivan, Nicholas P(2007). You can hear me now: How Micro loans and cell phones are connecting the world, San Francisco, CA: John Wilsey & Sans, 2007.

Reference

Ajzen, I (1991). The theory of planned behavior. Organizational behavior and human decision processes, 50(2), 179-211. doi: 10.1016/

0749.5978 (91) 90020-7.

Alba, Joseph W. and J. Wesley Hutchinson (1987). " Dimensions Of Consumer Expertise", Journal of consumer research, 13 March, 411-454.

Bailey, L., Mokhtarian, P.L. Little, A. (2008). The broader Connection Between Public Transportation, Energy Conservation And Greenhouse Gas Reduction, Report Prepared As Part Of TCRP Project J-11/Tasks Transit Cooperative Research Program, Transportation Research Board Submitted To American Public Transportation Association in http://www.apta.com/research/into/online/land_use.cfmi, accessed 17 April 2008.

Baucer, R,"Consumer Bhavior As Risk Taking , In Risk Taking And Information handling In Consumer Behavior", D. Coxceds Harvard University Press, Cambridge, Mass 1976.

Bogers, R. P., Brug, J. Van Assema, P., & Dagnetie, P.C. (2004) , Explaining fruit and vegetable consumption: The theory of planned behavior and misconception of personal intake level. Appetite, 42,157-166.

Bolton, Ruth N. (1998), " A Dynamic Model Of The Duration Of The Customer's Relationship With A Continuous Service Provider: The Role Of Satisfaction", Marketing Science, 17 (1), 45-65.

B.Shiv and A. Fedorikhin, " Heart And Min In Conflict: The Interplay Of affect And Cognition In Consumer Decision Making", J. Consumer Res., vol. 26, pp. 278-292, Dec. 1999.

Brown, K.W., Ryan, R.M. Reswell , J.D. (2007). Mindfulness: Theoretical Foundatins And Evidence For Its Salutary Effects. Psychological Inquiry, 18, 211-237.

Burke, R.R. : Behavioral effects of digital signage, J. Advertising Res. 49(2), 180-185 (2009).

Conner, M. & Abraham, C. (2001). Conscientiousness and the theory of planned behavior: Toward a more complete model of the antecedents of intention and behavior. Social psychology bulletin,

27, 1547-1561.

Cooper C. Mallon, K, Leadbetter S, Pollack L, Peipins (2005) , cancer internet search activity on a major search engine, United States 2001 to 2003, J Med Internet Res. 7(3): e36.

Cope, R. R. Cope and H. Davis (2008). Disney's virtual Queues: A strategic opportunity to co-brand services ? Journal of Business & economics research, vol. 6 no10, 13-20.

Cornelia, B.F. (1999) Rural development news, the North Central Regional Center For Rural Development vol. no 24 , IOWA.

David J. Nowak & Gordon M. Melsler (2016) " Air quality effects of urban trees and parks." National recreation and park association, USA.

De Hollander, A. E. M., J.M. Melse, Elebret & P. G.N. Kramers (1999), " An Aggregate public health indicator to represent the impact of multiple environmental exposures" Epidemiology: 606-617.

De Visser, R.O., & McDonnell, E.J. (2013). " Man points": Masculine capital and young men's health. Health psychology, 32(1), 5-14. doi:10. 1037/a0029045.

Dimson, Marsh & Staunton, London Business School (2005) In The Global Investment Returns Year Book, ABN Amro.

Dunn, J & A Neumsister (2002). Knowledge management in the Information age. E. business review, Fall , 37-45. Jounral of service, spring 2011, vol. 4, no1, De Grovte (2009).

Eysenbach G (2006) Infodemiology: Tracking flu- related searches on the web for syndromic surveillance. American Medical Informatics Associaion Annual Symposium Proceedings , Curran Associates, Red Hook, NY, pp. 244-248.

Ettredge M, Gerdes, J. Karuga , G (2005) Using web- based search data to predict macro-economic statistics. Commun ACM 48: 87-92.

Felce, D. and Perry, J. (1995). Quality of life: A contribution to its definition and measurement, vol. 16, no.1 pp: 51-74.

Feldman, Jack M. And John G. Lynch Jr. (1988), "Self-Generated Validity And Other Effects Of Measurement On Belife, Attitude, Intention And Behavior", Journal of applied psychology, 73(3),421-35.

Fiscal Policy And Long Term Growth, International Monetary Fund, IMF policy papers, Washington, D.C. Available from April, 2015, http://www.imf.org/external/pp/ppindex.aspx.

Fiese, M, Hofmann, W., & Wanke, M (2009). The impulsive consumer. Predicting consumer behavior with implicit reaction time measurement. In M. Wanke (ed.) Social psychology of consumer behavior (pp.335-364). New York, NY: Psychology press.

Fitzsimons, Gavan, J. And Vicki G. Morwitz (1996), " The Effect Of Measuring Intent On Brand-Level Purchase Behavior", Journal of consumer research, 23 (1), 1-11.

Hallerman , D. (2008) video Advertising Online: Spending And Pricing , New York. E-Marketer.

Harriet Griffey. (2010) The art of concentration, enhance focus, Reduce, stress and achieve move. Macmillan publishers ltd,Basinastoke and Oxford, London UK.

Helleman, D. (2008) Video Advertising Online: Spending And Pricing , New York, E-Marketer.

Huang, H.I. (2012). An empirical analysis of the strategic Management of competitive advantage: a case study of higher technical and vocational education in Taiwan (Doctoral dissertation, Victoria University).

Jamieson, Linda F. And Frank M. Bass (1989), " Adjusting Stated Intention Measures To Predict Trial Purchase Of New Products: A Comparison Of Models And Methods," Journal of marketing research, 26 (August), 336-45.

Kremers, S.P. J., De Bruijn, G.J., droomers, M., Van Lenthe, F. J., & Brug, J. (2005). Environmental interventions for selected dietary behaviors in adults. In J. Brug & F. J. Van Lenthe (eds.) ,

Environmental determinants and interventions for physical activity, nutrition and smoking: A review pp. 282-315. Rotterdam: Erasmus Medical Center.

Los Angeles Country Department Of public Health (2016), Country Health Ranking Model, Retrieved From www.countryhealthrankgings.org/our-approach. USA.

McGregor, S.L. T., & Goldsmith, E.B. (1998). Expanding our understanding of quality of life, standard of living and well-being. Journal of family and consumer science, 90(2), 2-6, 22.

McMichael, A.J. M. Mckee, J. Shkolnikov and T. Valkanen (2004), " Morality trends and setbacks, global convergence or divergence?", Lancet 363, 1155-1159.

Melse, J.M. & A.E. M. De Hollander (2001). " Human Health And The Environment", background document for the OECD Environmental Outlook, OECD, Paris.

Moschis, George p. & Roy, L. Moore (1979), " Decision making among the young. A socialization perspective " Journal of consumer research , 6 (September).

Mulligan, M. Banerjee, T & Thomas, N. (2008) ,European Paid Content And Activity Forecast, (2008 to 2013), Jupiter Research.

Peter, J., Ryan, M, M, " An Investigation Of Perceived Risk At The Brand Level, " Journal of marketing research, 13 May 1976, pp. 184-188.

Pieters, R., & Wedel, M. (2007). Goal Control Of Visual Attention To Advertising: The Yarbus Implication. Journal Of Consumer Research, 34, 224-233 (August).

Parasuaman, and Leonard L. Berry (1985), " Problems And Strategies In Sevices Marketing", Journal of marketing, 49 (Spring), 33-46.

R.C. Oliver, " When is consumer loyalty?" J.Marketing vol. 63, pp.33-44.1999.

Shostack, G. Lynn (1984), " Designing Services That Deliver", Harvard Business Review, 62 (January-February), 133-9.

Shostack, G. Lynn (1985), " Planning The Service Encounter ,in the service encounter" , John A. Czepiel, Michael R. Solomon, and Carol F. Suprenant, eds. New York: Lexington Books, 243-54.

Shostack, G. Lynn (1987), " Service Positioning Through, Structural Change", Journal of marketing, 51 (Janurary), 34-43.

Soloman, Michael R. (1985), "Packaging The Service Provider", Service Industries Journal , 5(1), 64-71.

Stevens, C.W. (1980), "K-MartStores Try New Look To Invite More Spending" The Wall Street Journal, Nov. 26, 29-35.

T. Ambler, A. Ioannides, And S. Rose, " Brand s On The Brain : Neuroimages Of Advertising ", Business Strategy rev., vol. 11, 3. pp. 17-30. 2000.

Westbrook, Robert A. (1980), " Intrapersonal affective influences on consumer satisfaction with products, " Journal of consumer research , 7 (June) 49-54.

Wiig, k.(1993). Knowledge management foundations: Thinking About thinking. How people and organizations create, represent and use knowledge vol.1 , of knowledge management series schema press: Arlington, TX.

World Health Organization (2003). Diet, nutrition and the prevention of Chronic diseases report of a joint WHO/FAO. expert consultation. Geneva: World Health Organization.

Wysocki, B. (1979), " Sight, Smell, Sound: They're all arms in retailer's arsenal" The Wall Street Journal, Nov. 17, 1979. 1-35.

Yale Center For Environmental Law And Policy (2006). Environmental Performance Index. Data available on-line at http://epi.yale.edu

Bibliography

Dimson, Marsh & Staunton, London Business School (2005) In The Global Investment Returns Year Book, ABN Amro.

THREE

CASES OF (AI) TECHNOLOGY APPLYING TO RAISE SERVICE PERFORMANCE

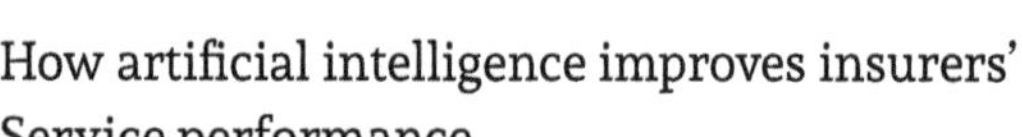

How artificial intelligence improves insurers'
Service performance

Can (AI) technology apply to insurance service industry to improve insurance service performance more efficient? Future (AI) robotic learning system can be applied to insurance service industry to help insurance clients to enquiry insurance policies or any insurance policies design matters in more efficient attitude when it can combine to internet technology together in possible. I shall explain the reasons as below:

Future (AI) learning system can be characterized by traditional software robotic process and tool is automation, enablement of high-volume, cubes-based activities. So, it seems to assist to insurance industry for these duties include: Simple rules-based process were the primary areas of focus in the insurance industry or making rules-based advisory services. Future (AI) learning system can think and it is characterized by the need to identify coded scenarios and critical incidents, it is intensive research and experimentation in (AI) and enablement of man-machine learning tools. It can reduce time need to bring these benefits to insurance industry, such as rapid adoption of technology in the form of IOT, code halos, big data, social listening as well as it is the foundational stage of insurers to enable (AI) learning systems to better understand insurance customers and what is happening in the market and develop into (AI) learning systems that think. Future (AI) learning systems that learn , can be characterized by self –learning, highly dynamic, non-rules, based adopting systems. SO, it can improve accuracy, piloting systems, and the evolution of commercial (AI) systems.

Insurance industry can apply systems that learn by use of (AI) aid human workers, development of the ecosystems for (AI) , evolution from man-machine learning to dynamic underwriting policies, virtual assistants, robotic-advisory and other viable use cases of (AI). So, future (AI) learning systems have possible to be applied to assist humans to underwrite policies, design and new policies plans for insurance medical or life or accident etc. different kinds of insurance policies target buyers' individual insurance needs. SO, it will be one logic mind high technologic tool to assist insurers to reduce time to design any new insurance policies to satisfy every potential insurance buyers' needs more accurate.

Can (AI) learning systems reduce medical insurance buyers' claim time, each medical policy evaluation check and confirmation processing time reducing, even assists to insurance agents to answer medical insurance buyers' enquiry time reducing or assist human insurers to design different kinds of unique beneficial medical policy plans to attract medical insurance buyers to choose to buy the insurance company's medical policies more easily? I shall indicate these cases to explain why (AI) learning system can be applied to insurance industry to do any logic tasks. (AI) robotic thinking and learning and doing learning systems can apply to driverless cars. Even, it can be applied to healthcare organizations aspect, organizations are using (AI) solution to enhance diagnoses, real-time patient monitoring and medication treatments. IN fact, many medical or healthcare organizations are applying this (AI) learning systems to build virtual assistants for doctors to improve medical service performance for patients. Moreover, medical product firms and applying (AI) fueled customer and insights to design different fashion of medical products to attract medical product clients to choose to buy their medical products.

Hence, it seems that (AI) learning systems can be applied (AI) experimentation and implementation to any service or manufacturing organizations in order to raise productive efficiencies or improve service performance. It will bring beneficial customer demand, cost pressure and the need to maintain or expand their market.

How does apply (AI) learning systems to improve insurer' service performance to any insurance products buyers. In the future (AI) learning, thinking and doing systems can assist human workers rather than displaying them in insurance industry in two areas:

On underwriting aspect, (AI) learning systems can be used to perform research, aggregate, refine and present required information to underwriters, allowing them to focus core underwriting activities . SO, (AI) learning systems can concentrate on insurance research activities aspect in any insurance firms.

On advisory services aspect, (AI) learning systems can be virtual assistants to assist insurers to manage the low-value activities of advisors, such as lead management, scheduling, planning , licensing etc. value –add daily activities to reduce insurers to spend extra time to do not important tasks in order to improve service performance for their insurance clients. Even, (AI) learning systems can be self-learning to underwrite for any insurance policies and assist insurers to evaluate whether how much insurance claim is the accurate number as well as evaluate whether the insurance buyer is reasonable to claim the compensation amount when accident occurrence or sickness occurrence. It can make the claim judgement more accurate than human's judgement. For long term benefits, instead of (AI) learning system can help insurance companies to improve client service experience. IT can also bring revenue expansion to the insurance firm organization. The real-time learning and adaptive capabilities of (AI) can be provided a ready platform for insurers to explore new insurance product lines, geographies and client segments. Insurance organizations can increase their ability to manage , such as information search, data management, and process automation by (AI) learning system assistants. Moreover, (AI) learning systems can help insurers to give options to attempt to answer insurance clients' queries and complaints in short time. SO, insurers can develop real-time (AI) capabilities to help them to handle any market challenges better than their competitors in global insurance businesses in order to achieve improvement of customer service performance to let insurance clients to experience daily. So, insurers with (AI) capabilities will help them better to improve customer service performance to let them to experience their efficient insurance sale and enquiry service to their organizations.

However, insurance is an emotion-driven industry. But, (AI) learning system is one machine. How and why can (AI) learning system help human emotion-driven insurance service sale organization to influence insurance clients' emotion to be positive more than negative? It is one interesting question to be explained. When one insurance company grows to mature stage, it won't have effort to make initial steps with chat bots, many have also advanced to robotic advisory. Based on organizational maturity and insurance market also reaches the insurance customer number reducing stage. Due to any country has have many family owns at least one insurance policy. So, it will influence every family's insurance need to be reduced.

However, (AI) system new technology is the best method to assist insurers to predict whether who will be the potential insurance customer target groups in order to help the insurance organizations to predict more accurate every family's emotion to find whose unfound insurance needs. As a result, future insurance organizations can apply (AI) learning systems to bring these benefits, they include: attaining rapid growth through channel and potential insurance customer prediction touchpoint of different kinds of insurance need expansion; employing operational intelligent to optimize resource overhead and improve insurance customer new fresh experience insight from (AI) learning system service participation to the insurance organization, modernizing technology to solve legacy problems, such as scalability , service turnaround times etc. So, the most influential advantage is that (AI) learning system can help future insurance organizations to find the best insurance methods to solve insurance customer complains or service challenges. Because insurance is an emotion business, when the insurance client had chosen to buy the insurance firm any kinds of insurance , it does not guarantee that the insurance client has none any complains. SO, the insurance company will encounter reasonable or unreasonable complains often. (AI) learning system's strengths includes that it can find the best method to help any insurance firm to give recommendation to attempt to solve their insurance customers' complains in the shortest time. If the (AI) learning system can really help the insurance firm to find the best methods to solve any insurance clients' complains or enquiries to let every insurance client to feel more acceptable to compare human insurers' insurance customer service feedbacks are more better or satisfactory to let them to feel. Then, I believe that the insurance clients must feel the insurance firm can improve its customer service more efficient and satisfactory. For example, chat bot is one find of insurance product personal financial tracker tool for every insurance customer. Chat bot is starting with a enabled. It is one personal financial tracker and advisor (starting with a rules-based configuration) to target prospects and insurance customers. Thus, through the use of rules-enables easily configurable decision and process engineers, insurers can not only save on resources , but also

ensure more efficient marketing, lead management and insurance sales efforts, all at minimal cost to the insurance company.
So, (AI) learning system can help insurers to enter digital journey. IT (information technological) techniques to predict potential insurance client's insurance needs more accurate. (AI) learning system can be applied to social media presence, mobile solutions to the insurance organization's target market. Hence, (AI) learning system and digital social media technology can help the insurer to predict whose knowledge of potential insurance customers insurance product needs and insurance consumption behaviors more accurate. The (AI) learning system and digital social media technology can make multiple channels and touchpoints of any kinds of insurance sale and service, e.g. life, accident, sickness, travelling, professional duty , e.g. construction firm accident claim, lawyer etc. professional occupation negligence claim etc. reasonable claim rate method which conclude more accurate and reasonable claim result to compare human's judgement in order to solve challenges to satisfy the insurance target customer and let them to experience firm (AI) learning system and social media internet tool both application to any future insurance organizations. For another example, of basic (AI) pilot solutions that can be built and tested in a short time span with a relatively low rick of investment to share insurance management's daily tasks, e.g. virtual sales assistants that manage basic routine work (e-mails, meetings, lead search etc.) , automated algorithms for needs analysis that can be deployed across all insurance customer-facing channel, thus insurance (AI) learning system is such in insurance management's sale assistant staff or robotic-advisor to help them to solve not predictive insurance clients' complains or enquiries in any time efficiently. This (AI) learning system technology can effectively solve raise insurers' point-of-sale capabilities, straight-through processing or satisfying the insurance customer's individual insurance policy's enquiries or complains, discovering possible routes or up and cross sell through better insurance sale methods.

In fact, some insurers have already adopted (AI) capabilities , they include: Swiss Reinsurance company is working with IBM Watson to develop a range of underwriting solutions and achieve accurate risk pricing; Insurify . com enables insurance customers to generate price quotes by texting a photo of their license plate. Insurify's patent-pending license plate option Evia (short for expert virtual insurance agent) is built on processing . IT does not require a mobile app. To be download or installed. Insurance customers can simply text a photo of their license plate when they buy vehicle accident insurance. Manulife has transformed its authentication mechanism from the conventional password and PIN system to voice recognition. Through a partnership with voice recognition leader durance communications, Manulife can analyze unique voice characteristics to create individual "voiceprint" for insurance customers. When insurance customers call in to access their insurance buyer accounts, their voice is compared with a stored voiceprint. If these is a match , access is granted. Customers at Buyonic insurance agency in Austin. TX can apply (AI) learning system machine to bring the most accurate insurance policy claim rate and issues insurance policies on the spot, when answering phones and making robotics (AI) learning voice system. Zest Finance takes an entirely different approach to underwriting by combining (AI) machine learning technique and data analysis with traditional credit scoring. Micro soft and Gaffcy Healthcare have collaborated on a pilot to deploy (AI) learning machines in Gaffef's claims automation and processing engine immediately. USAA added Nuance communications' virtual assistant (Nina) to its existing mobile customer service apps to enable speech recognition, text-t-t-speech, voice biometrics and NPL capabilities. All of these insurance companies (insurers) need to equip (AI) learning system themselves with the ability to gather specific information from various sources. They also need a highly integrated and digitalized environment together in order to let (AI) capabilities to provide insurer ready components across functional areas, such as new insurance policies business, different kinds of insurance sales and distribution and insurance customer service from (AI) learning machine system digital speech-to text platform and brings sentiment analysis capabilities to achieve excellent myriad insurance customer-serving purposed.

In conclusion, future (AI) learning system can be really attempted to apply to insurer businesses to help them to feel real human customer service voice feedback feeling when insurance clients phone call to enquire these (AI) learning system any questions concern their insurance issues or complain any insurance issues at home. Then, the (AI) learning system will find the most accurate or reasonable solutions to answer their enquiries or complains in order to satisfy their insurance demand in the shortest time immediately. However, above all functions are not only one kind of capability to (AI) learning system, future (AI) learning system can be applied to many new different kinds of new functions to insurance service industry. SO, it seems that future (AI) learning systems have effort to help human customer service staffs to improve customer service performance in future insurance industry.

Can Artificial intelligence apply to digital-Transformation on jobs to raise productivity

Future, digital transformative technologies will how impact on economies and societies as well as how (AI) utilization of vast amounts of data to be applied to digital transformative technology. I believe that when (AI) is applied to digital transformative technology which will bring positive impacts on productivity for many firms, but it has not yet translated into stronger productivity growth at the economy –wide level. Larger impacts could result from digital technologies to all firms, notably to small and medium sized enterprises.

However, firms expected that (AI) technology and digital transformative technology can help them to raise productivity , which need have greater investments in critical complementary assets, such as firm-level skills, organizational change and process innovation as well as support for future structural change to enable the growth of new business models and digitally-intensive businesses. However, the (AI) technology is applied to digital transformative technological changes creates significant uncertainty about their future directions and impacts. Indeed, predictions about technological timelines are often inaccurate and over estimate of their short-time impacts is common.

How to achieve (AI) and the internet of things (IOT) and black chain technologies to raise productivities? It depends on large data sets and a range od digital technologies. Strong potential to improve the design implementation and evaluation of organizational policies (strategies of any firms expect to apply (AI) and internet technology combination to raise productivities.

Nowadays, global societies and private organizational firms considerate human centric (AI) needs for societies, and for further information sharing need, deepen the understanding of the potential effects of (AI) technologies on society and economies, ethics, privacy. Job creation issues. Instead of (AI) is constrained to the digital world, with significant activity to influence , such as transport and machinery industry aspects, future (AI) technology can also be applied to service industry, such as healthcare and finance, education and training system in order to raise young people and adults right skills performance and productive efficiencies in an (AI)-enabled environment.

Hence, (AI) transformative and digital technological combination can impact those aspects to influence productivities. On gender influence aspect, Gender is particularly important in ensuring technological transformation of production change working environment. Female and male workers need to learn how to apply (AI) and digital transformative technology to work in offices or factories to strengthen their position in the labor market and in driving the digital transformation in order to achieve the aim of raising productivities. On skills safeguard against the risk of automation influence aspect, fewer than 5% of worker with a tertiary degree are at a high risk of losing their job, due to automation compared to 40% of workers with a lower secondary degree.

In future (AI) and digital technological working environment , workers needed to be equipped with a wide set of skills to be equipped with a wide set of skills as well as non-cognitive and social skills (notably information and communication technology (ICT) skills, science, technology, engineering ad mathematics (STEM) skills, and self-organization skills). Future, (AI) and digital technologies can potentially also promote social inclusion by creating education, offer-new opportunities for skills development, enhance access to healthcare industry or improve access to free and low-cost information, knowledge, and data to help organizations to improve service performance or raise productivity.

How (AI) and digital technological working environment influence job changed for employees. When, it is uncertainty about the speed of changes, it is clear that the types of jobs that are being created are not the same as those that are being lost. Moreover, the workers are affected by job loss in declining activities may not be those benefitting from the new job opportunities in any organizations. The middle –skilled jobs declining and low and high skilled jobs growing. Low –skilled workers are mostly likely to bear the costs of digital transformation, but are currently the least likely to receive training. So, the employers need to apply (AI) and digital technology to raise productivities which will influence some low-skilled workers will lose jobs, unless they can learn how to apply this new (AI) and digital technology to assist them to work in any working environments.

Better understanding the likely scope of the digital transformation and (AI) technology combination is needed to any organizations including: the growth of the big economy, or the impacts on productivity , the growing role of data, including in traditional trade is a particularly important area where sound data , i.e. data on data flow that is lacking . Although, there are still large difference in digital intensity, every firm in every sector in the economy is now being affected by the digital transformation, expanding its scope and its potential benefits. All organizations need to learn how to apply digital technology to assist whose workers to work efficiently in factories or offices in beginning. When they can learn how to apply digital technology to work. Then, they can learn how to apply (AI) technology and digital technology together to work together in order to achieve raising productivities or improve performance aims. For example, data combined with (AI) and digital technological innovation is online activity and networked things generate " big data" which feed machine learning that enables (AI), to lead to advances in intelligent machines (robotics, automated vehicles) as well as new techniques in science which can be further innovation. The growth of the volume, variety data and the ability to analyze and use it is a significant departure from the past and it causes new factor of production that argues traditional capital and labor, but unique properties of its own to be applied to office or factory manufacturing work environment in order to achieve the raising of productivity or improve performance in possible.

Why does (AI) and digital transformative combination technologies raise productivity growth or improve service performance? From 1995 to 2004 year, US experienced an acceleration in productivity growth, largely reflecting gains associated with the diffusion of ICT technologies. From the early to mid-2000 year onward, productivity growth has slowed down. The potential impacts of the ongoing digital transformation on productivity also need to consider in the context of this long term slowdown. When, the precise reasons for today's productivity remain difficult to a number of factors are likely to contribute as below factors:

The first factor that has limited the impacts of digital transformation is the state of diffusion of digital technologies across the economy. When, many firms now have across to broadband networks, the use of more advanced digital tools and application with firms still differs greatly across countries. Moreover, these are important differences between rapid technological change, advanced technologies are initially only adopted by some leading firms and then only later diffuse to all firms as the technologies because more established new business models grow, such as applying digital and (AI) technological combine method to raise productivity growth is caused and costs fall.

Consequently, these is large demand between what can be automated from a technical point of view and what may already be implemented by frontier firms and what is actually being achieve to raise productivity growth aim. So, (AI) and digital transformative technology influence future raising productivity growth or improving service aim achievement for many manufacturing and service industry demand.

The second factor indicator that the available evidence suggests that the wide-spread benefits of digitalization productivity are not enough. Firms expect to help strengthen investment (in tangible and intangible assets), e.g. (AI) technology. The same time, there are now starting to experience labor shortages, e.g. in certain technical occupations, such as data scientists. Due to the technological change is fast and growing demand for productivity growth has been increasing. SO, it will influence future (AI) robotic learning system and digital technological combination to be applied to manufacturing and service industries' needs to be raised. Due to many firms expect to find methods to raise productivity growth in order to reduce production costs.

However, (AI) and digital technological development can cause multiple forms of disruption, from shifts in demand for workforce skills to changes in market structure, the need for new business models, new patterns of trade and investment. The (AI) and digital potentially transformative technologies can create new inventions, e.g. from quantum computing and advanced energy storage to new forms of 3D printing, big data analytics and neuro-technologies. These new product creative industries must lead the new product manufacturers to expect to learn how to apply (AI) and digital technology to raise productivity growth when their manufacturing processes.

IN fact, (AI) is the ability of learning machine and system to acquire and apply knowledge and carry out intelligent behavior. Early efforts to develop (AI) centered on defining rules that software could use to perform a tack, such systems would work in speech recognition, (AI) skill. Increase in computational power, new statistical methods and advances in big data, have brought major breakthroughs to the field of (AI), especially in " vertical " (AI) like automated vehicles as opposed to " general". (AI) with machine learning algorithms that identify complex patterns in large data sets. Software applications can perform tasks and simultaneously learn how to improve productive performance. Hence, (AI) can be combined to digital world to work together with advanced in electrical engineering, it has robots to perform cognitive task in the physical world. (AI) will enable robots to adapt to new working environments with no reprogramming. Also, (AI) enabled robots will become increasingly central to logistics and manufacturing, complementing and sometimes displacing human labor in many production processes.

Future (AI) will also be developed to apply to service industry, e.g. healthcare, entertainment, marketing and finance industries. Even, future (AI) that recognizes human facial expressions and emotions could help to deliver some public services and possibly educational services. Future an essential factor achieve benefits of (AI) is the provision of reliable energy and communication networks, including for the IOT. Therefore, laws and legal frameworks may need to be considered before many of the benefits of (AI) can be bad in fields, such as transportation and healthcare industries. All above of these industries will need (AI) technology and digital technologies combination to help future manufacturing or service industries both to raise their productivity growth or improve service performance in order to reduce cost or provide more service satisfactory feeling to clients in their manufacturing processes or service processes in any manufacturing or service environments.

Can robots raise productive
efficiency to logistic industry

Can (AI) raise productive efficiency to logistic industrial sector? Technological progress in the fields of big data, algorithmic development, connectivity , cloud computing have made the performances, accessibility and costs of (AI) more favorable. Logistics is beginning to become an (AI)- driven industry, but it has also encountered challenges to overcome and opportunities to exploit. As in other industries, (AI) will extend human efficiency in terms of reach quality and speed by eliminating routine work. This will allow logistic workforces to focus in more meaningful and impactful work.

How can (AI) raise productive growth efficiency or fast manufacturing speed to logistic industry? (AI) can be defined as human intelligence exhibited by machines, syustems that approximate, replicate, automate and eventually improve on human thinking . It owns the ability to perceive , understand, learn , problem solve and reason. Whereas, (AI) is a system or device intended to amount with intelligence, machine learning is a more specific to taken in formation, usually within a specific domain, and learn from what they have been given. These learning systems draw on the ability to evaluate and categorize received data and then draw inferences from this. The output of this process is an insight decision or conclusion.

(AI) technology consists of sensing, components, processing components and learning components. SO, (IA) has this analytical process: (AI) can have deep learning ability to improve to process and understand unstructured data, e.gf. text, image, sound , then data gathered continuously from the environment, sensors and online behavior and data is aggregated. Next, machine learning framework begins to process data, patterns and trends are revealed, generated insight. Finally, the (AI) learning system takes different actions to drive value. New action is used as input to improve self-learning of system. IT is any (AI)'s full learning cycle in (AI) analytical process.

How can (AI) apply its supervised learning skills to raise productive efficiency to logistic industry? The processing and learning components and training techniques to (AI) includes" Once an (AI) system has collected data from sensing, it processes this information by applying a learning framework to generate insight from the data. IN addition to the similarities that exist between human intelligence and (AI) , strong parallels have also been observed between how humans and (AI) learning systems.

In the future, (AI) can be such a supervised learning machine man to supervise logistic workers and control and manage them how to deliver goods in warehouses more efficient. Even, they can replace human logistic workers to do their logistic tasks in warehouses. What is (AI) supervised learning system mean : It is learning that takes place when an (AI) –enabled system is directly informed by humans. I shall explain it as doctor case, A doctor who evaluates x-ray images to detect cancer risk, he/she can feed whose expert input images into an (AI) learning system to facilities supervised learning or when the (AI) learning system sorts through x-ray images for a doctor to review and approve in an effort to help improve the learning of the (AI) learning system. So, it seems that (AI) learning system can be applied to do any supervising tasks. When, (AI) robotic machines are applied to logistic warehouse environment, it can be one artificial intelligent supervisor to check any products whether are delivered to the exact locations or shelfs as well as the number of products whether it is accurate to be prepared to delivery to the outsider accurate destinations before all goods are already sent out from the warehouses. For example, Amazon publish company paper book buyers need to buy paper books , when they pay visa payment and every reader choose the right topic book from its website, when they choose to buy the topic of paper book, then Amazon publish will send the reader 's the topic book choice to its warehouse. When the logistic worker know what the topic of the paper book is sold, then the (AI) learning system will record the topic of the book and the country address of the paper book buyer to already to print the topic of paper book and send to the book buyer's address. Due to , there are many different countries paper book buyers who had chosen the different topic books to buy from amazon publish website. For example, if there are five hundred different countries book buyers who had paid visa to buy different topic books from Amazon publish website in the same day. Then , Amazon publish needs to deliver these five hundred different countries paper book buyers overseas address and the warehouse workers need to print all these five hundred different topic paper books in the same time in order to deliver all these five hundred paper books to their overseas home within two days. If Amazon publish has none of (AI) learning system to help it to record this five hundred different topic paper book buyers' overseas correct addresses and the accurate topic of every book. Then , I believe that Amazon publish has no more confidence to print the accurate different paper book right topic number and record all the different countries paper book buyers' overseas home addresses and names in order to print and deliver to them from warehouse within two days. SO, (AI) learning system can help this electronic publishing firm to record all these five hundred different countries paper book buyers' addresses and every paper book topic in its centered logistic system efficiently and effectively. Amazon publish can reduce some warehouse workers number , due to it has (AI) learning system to help it to record all paper book buyer's address and name and book topic clearly. Even, (AI) robotic machine men can help it to deliver any book to the accurate shelf location in order to delivery the right topic of every book to post to the right country's book buyer's address before all these five hundred different topic books are already posted to their overseas addresses by air planes. SO, (AI) learning system and robotics can help this publisher to manage and supervise all warehouse workers how to put these five hundred paper books to the different shelves locations more accurate in this day in warehouse. If it lacks(AI) learning system and robotic warehouse machine man to assist its warehouse workers to work in warehouse. It will increase the risk to post the wrong topic book to the wrong book buyer's address.

However, in logistic industry (AI) learning system applying key challenge facing the progress of (AI) is that logistic industry users do not trust it, because they still feel (AI) learning system can't supervise workers to deliver and distribute any products to achieve 100% accuracy in warehouses confidently. So I recommend that , the returns on (AI) investments are already improving in logistic industry and the growth in customer –facing commercial areas clearly indicates the use of (AI) learning systems and robotics in industrial sectors, such as logistic is quickly approaching. Furthermore, future many logistic companies depend on networks both physical and increasingly digital, which must function to bring these benefits, such as high products volumes and accurate numbers delivery, learn asset allocation, low margins and time-sensitive deadlines. SO, (AI) learning system and robotic machine men can offer logistic companies the ability to optimize network to degrees of efficiency and accurate number of different kinds of product deliveries, such as Amazon publish warehouse different topic printed books are delivered to overseas readers case. (AI) can also help the logistic industry to definite warehouse delivery behaviors and practices, taking operations from reactive to proactive , planning from forecast to prediction ,process from manual to autonomous, and services from standardized to personalized, warehouse delivery needs . For IBM computer products warehouse delivery case example, (AI) learning system can apply network to help IBM computer manufacturing workers to grow productivity and effectiveness of individual knowledge workers. They can be IBM manufacturing workers' assistants to assist them to manufacture any kinds of computer products in warehouse more efficiently. It can bring reducing time spending to manufacturers and (AI) robotic machine manufacturers both manufacture every computers' parts or components together in IBM warehouses. It will bring the benefits include: reducing manufacturing spending time, high productivity growth, high efficiency, avoiding manufacturing errors occurrence in IBM computer every manufacturing process.

The use of (AI) engineering and manufacturing signals a departure from the purely digital world. It can now shape the physical world around us. The manufacturing conglomerate general electric is ways to deliver power, energy and air travel. Part of the answer may be to use (AI) to inform, the production requirements and manage the continuous operation of heavy machinery to supervise products distribution, supply chain into one intelligent system in logistic warehouses. The system is connected to an intelligent order management system. Once the problem is understood and the required parts are identifies from the images , the correct parts order can be placed automatically . Finally, if specialist intervention is needed, the smart manufacturing platform can check the technician's schedule and suggest the best times for maintenance in warehouses. So, A(I) learning system can be also applied to supervise and manage warehouse works in warehouses.

Why can (AI) learning system raise productivity growth in logistic industry warehouses? (AI) learning system can be value add chain by automating existing business processes, uncovering new chain add value from data and augmenting logistic management decisions and actions . The ability to analyze levels of data that are beyond human comprehension allows logistic businesses to personalize, fast speed logistic experiences, customize products and logistic deliver services and identify productivity growth opportunities with a speed and precision that has never been positive before.

Hence, future (AI) learning system may be applied to those logistic industries , such as below:

On accurate demand forecasting beneficial aspect, in retail industry improved 1 to 2 % logistic speed to transport , improvement using machine learning to anticipate fruit and vegetable sales, 20% stock reduction using deep learning to predict e-commerce purchases, fewer product returns per year; in electric utilities industry, it can achieve objective to cut 10% in natural electricity usage by using deep learning to predict power demand and supply; on higher productivity and maintenance and repairs aspect, in retail industry , (AI) learning system has 30% reduction of stocking time using autonomous vehicles in warehouses; in electric utilities industry,

(AI) learning system has 20% energy production increase using machine learning and smart sensors to optimize assets' yield as well as 10 to 20% improvement by using machine learning to enhance predictive maintenance , automate fault prediction and increase capital productivity; in manufacturing industry, (AI) learning system has 30% increase of machines delivery time using machine learning to determine timing of products' transfer and 3 to 5% production yield can be improved.

In conclusion, future (AI) learning system can enable massive productivity gains for logistic industry automating their process. Logistic industry can combine with the industrial internet of things, achieve learning can predict anomalies and sensor data, image videos and audio data and therefore reduce losses in warehouses. Moreover, manufacturers for instance are using machine learning and other (AI) techniques to better predict failure and thus to reduce maintenance costs in warehouses.

Applying artificial intelligence and machine learning to improve service performance in financial services

Future, predicting artificial intelligence (AI) and machine learning technology will be rapidly adopted for a range of application in the financial services industry. I shall explain how to apply (AI) to improve service performance for any kinds of financial service clients.

In the future, (AI) will be increased to supply to satisfy different kinds of financial service industry to satisfy whose needs to raise service performance. The needs include: Financial institutions will use (AI) and machine learning methods to access credit quality to price and market insurance contracts and to automate client interaction. They are optimizing scarce capital will (AI) and machine learning techniques, as well as back-testing models and analyzing the market impact of trading larger positions. Hedge funds, brokers deal etc. firms are using (AI) and machine learning to find signals for higher and uncorrlated returns and optimize trading execution , both public and private financial institutions may use (AI) techniques for regulatory compliance, surveillance, data quality assessment and fund detection.

Why and how (AI) and learning system can improve service performance for any financial institutions. The more efficient processing of information for example in credit decisions, financial markets, insurance contracts and customer interaction may contribute to a more efficient financial system and it can help improve regulatory compliance and increase effectiveness. At the same time, network effects and scalability may give rise to third-party dependencies.

Applications of (AI) nd machine learning can be variable to meet various financial institutions' needs. The uses of (AI) and machine learning will help financial institutions' clients to reduce personal or financial risk, e.g. data privacy, conduct risks. Also, adequate testing and training of tools with data and feedback mechanisms is important to ensure applications do what they are intended to do. So, (AI) and machine learning technology can be applied to financial industry as these aspects: customer -focused application, operation-focused uses application, trading and portfolio management application aspects.

(AI) big data is used broadly to storage and analysis of large and / or complicated data sets using a variety of techniques including (AI). The analytics often related to the amount of unstructured or sem-structured data in data sets. The technology can be applied to help any financial institutions to improve service performance. Machine learning may be defined aas a method of designing a sequence of actions to solve a problem, known as algorithms, which optimise automatically through experience and with limited or no human intervention. These techniques can be used find patterns in large amounts of data (big data analytics) from increasingly diverse and innovations sources to help any financial institutions for be supervised to learn to be improve service performance from every time the client's financial service to absorb financial service experiences in order to achieve to raise financial service performance or service level for any financial institutions.

Why can (AI) deep learning algorithms be applied to financial service industry to raise service performance? For encoding the concept of a car case example, It is from a series of discovering generalisable concepts, such as encoding images. So, an investor might deploy an alogorithm to gather data to predict retail store sale numbers in a particular period. An alogorithm can recognise cars to count the number of cars in a retail parking lot of from a satellite image in order to infer a likely stores, sale figure for a particular period.

As applicationing to financial service case, natural language processing of deep learning algorithms can allow computers to read and produce written texr or when combined with voice recognition to read and produce spoken language. This allows financial institutions to automate financial service factors previously requiring to automate financial service factoring previosly requiring mannual intervention. (AI) big data technology can also help financial institutions to decide whether the firm has ability to pay back loan and interest . When it borrow loan from the financial institution. This technology will help the financial institution to gather past data to evaluate and analyze its credit rate report more accurate than manual judgement. Even, it can help the financial institutions to evaluate how much loan amount can be lent to the firn more accurate in order to decide its loan pay back period and load and interest calculation amount to conclude the accurate lending loan service and interest charge amount to the firm (loan borrower) more confident.

Another example , it might be to automatically apply (AI) big data technology to read sale report or estimate an unrated company's intitial credit client's financial situation in order to evaluate whether the financial loan service firm has effort to pay its loan and interest to the financial company in the particular period in possib.e. Since cloud computing and internet technology created this new website technology can combine to (AI) deep learning

algorithms.
In order to collect big amount, big data concerns the financial company's client's financial transactions in short time, e.g. big data on the scale of every single credit card transaction interconnectedness of information technology resources with cloud computing with whose big data can now be organized and analyzed. Using big data sets of this size and complexity and with the increase in cloud computing power, machine learning algorithms client's financial situation results more accurate than every financial consultant individual judgement.
In conclusion, human intelligence learning machine can replace or assist human financial consultants' some logic or complexity financial analysis tasks in any financial service organization's departments in order to reduce their workloads to achieve to improve financial service performance to their clients more satisfactory or effectively. Even future (AI) learning machine and big data and internet combination technology can bring these benefits to any financial service organizations, such as faster processor speeds, lower hardware cost, and better access to computer power via cloud computing services. If the financial service organization chose to apply (AI) machine learning technology to share financial service workers' tasks in different departments. It will bring to improve better service performance and reduce cost for the financial service organization in possible.

Can artificial intelligence raise
productivity growth efficiency
in industrial sector

When (AI) robotic technology is applied to any industrial sectors, instead of replacing or helping labor workers to do some simple tasks to share their workload beneficial aspect, whether it can really help them to raise productivity growth or work efficiency in any industrial working environments. Which are subindustries the most strongly affected by the automation potential of (AI)? How can managers of industrial players cooperate with (AI) and workers work efficiently in order to achieve to raise productivity growth aim?

Future (AI) technology can bring two aspects of benefits in industrial sector manufacturing operations and business processes both aspects as below:

On manufacturing operations aspect, predictive maintenance is enhanced by (AI) allows for better prediction and avoidance of machine failure by combining data from advanced internet of things (IOT) sensors and maintenance logs as well as external sources. So, asset productivity can increase of up to 20% are possible , and overall maintenance costs may be reduced up to 10%; collaborative aware robots will improve production through based on (AI) enabled human machine interaction in labor-intensive settings. Therefore, productivity increases up to 20% are feasible for certain-tasks, even when tasks are not fully automatable; yield enhanccement in manufacturing powered by (AI) will result in decreased scrap rates are testing costs by linking various across machinery groups and sub-processes, e.g. in the semi-conductor industry, the use of (AI) can lead to a reduction in yield detraction by up to 30%. Moreover, automated quality testing can be realized using (AI). By employing advanced image recognition techniques for visual inspection and fault detections productivity increases of up to 50% are possible. Specificantly, (AI) based visual inspection based on image recognition may increase defect detection rates up to 90% as compared to human inspection.

On business processes beneficial aspect, (AI) enhanced supply chain management greatly improves forecasting accuracy when increasing and optimizing stock replenishment. Reductions between 20 and 50% in forecasting errors are feasible. So, lost sales due to products not being available can be reduced by up to 65% and inventory reductions of 20% to 50% are achieved; The application of machine learning to enable high-performance R&D projects has large potential. So, research and research cost reductions of 10 to 15% and time-do-market improvements up to 10% are expected. Finally, business support function automation will ensure improvements in both process quality and efficiency. Automation

rates of 30% are possible across functions. For the specific example IT service desks, automation rates of 90% are expected.
Can (AI) automatin technology innovate the future of production? Trends towards higher levels of automation causes greater speed and precision of producton as well as reduced exposure to dangerous tasks for employees. New production technologies could help overcome the stagnant productivity and make may for more valued added activity in production sector.
Exciting advances in the internet of things, artificial intelligence, advanced robotics, wearables and 3 D printint are transforming what, where and how products are designed, manufactured, assembled, distributed, consumed, service after purchase, even reused. They affect and alter all end-to-end steps of the production process and as a result, transform the products that consumers demand, the factory process and the management of global supply chains, addition to industry pecking orders and countries' access. So, future (AI) robotic technology will be applied to those production sectors. They include 80% of wearables market and almost 70% of industrial 3D printing units. Other specific industries with automotive, electronics and aerospace being early adopter in most cases to apply (AI) robotic technology to help their workers to work more efficient and to achieve productivity growth.
In fact, competitive production is demanded to reduce cost in higher manufacturing cost environmeents. (AI) robotic technology will have possible to help manufacturers to reduce cost, e.g. when the production environment occurs in the capital-intensive sectors with high transportation costs . So, if the manufacturer does not choose to apply (AI) robotic manufacturing technology to help it to assist workers to manufacture in factory. Then, it's traditional manufacturing technology will negatively impact white and blue-collar workers on the factory floor if societies do not ready their workforce for the new (AI) robotic skill sets and put in place transition mechanisms to ease negative impacts.
Future, (AI) robotic technology will bring these advantages to manufacturing industry's production process: Mapping a

comprenhensive technology to impact one or more aspects of global production systems. Exercises followed to prioritize and focus analysis on deemed to have the broadest applicability across value chain elements; a foresight series was created for each production (AI) robotic technology. Capturing current technical readiness and adoption levels across (AI) robotic production processes, manufacturing industries focusing on the impact of the (AI) robotic production technologies by understanding the connections between (AI) robotic manufacturing technology and traditional non-(AI) robotic manufacturing technology and they compete in solving firm by social production process problems and by bringing the positive production method impact on the factory floor and on firms, industries, societies and individual manufacturing needs.

For example, advanced robotics can be applied to 3 D printing technological manufacturing copied product tasks from digital -physical transformation. So, (AI) robotics can replace workers to do any 3D printing tasks to copy any products. The benefits to change the factory's physical location to be small areas, high speed network, raising producers' revenues (new offering, business models) and reducing cots (selling, administrative expenses, logistic etc.) , less long term investments and capabilities to achieve 3 D printing product increasing number in efficient (AI) robotic working speed. Although , it is possible to destroy factory labor worker 3 D printing product job, but it can create new 3 D printing (AI) robotic controller working jobs to be technicians to teach (AI) robotic machines to learn how to use 3 D printer to manufacture any copied products. The most important benefit of 3D robotic machines replacing labor 3D printing labors that is the manufacturer can reduce labor 3 D printing worker number, due to the manufacturer applies (AI) robotic to assist the 3D printing workers to fo every step of manufacturing copied product tasks. So, the 3D printing (AI) robotic machine labors can replace all 3 D printing labor workers to do every step to apply 3 D printers to manufacture every copied product. Otherwis, the 3 D printing copied product manufacture will employ the (AI) robotic technicians to control and supervise and teach the (AI) robotic 3 D printing product machines to learn how to use the 3 D printers to do every step to manufacture different kinds of copied products to sell in the market. Hence, the 3 D printer copied product manufacture will reduce labors and salary when it applies 3 D printing robotic machine labors to replace labor workers to finish every printing step to manufacture different kinds of copied products in factory. for example, when the 3 D printing technicians had taught the robotic machine to learn how to apply 3 D printer to manufacture a copied vehicle's motor engine. Then, the (AI) robotic machine had learnt how to apply the 3D printer to manufacture different kinds of copied vehicle motor engines in every step. It is possible that the (AI) robotic machine 3D printing skills will be improved more better to compare human 3 D printing workers' skills as well as its 3D printing vehicle motor engine copied product manufacturing speed will also faster than human 3D printing worker's printing copied manufacturing product's speed. Consequently, it will bring positive benefits to any kinds of vehicle engine products productivity number growth to sell different kinds of vehicle engines to vehicle sellers to different country vehicle sale market in order to raise its global vehicle engine sale market competitive effirt and revenue. So, (AI) robotic machine seems really raise productivity growth when it is applied to manufacturing industry.

Why is (AI) learning system the best tool to be applied to manufacturing industry? In fact, future (AI) robotic machine will be one kind of intangible capital to manufacturing organizations to help them to innovate, adjustment costs, organizational changes to be better and new manufacturing skills are needed for successful in every production process.

Historically, most computer programs were created by codifying human knowledge, step-by-step, mapping inputs to outputs by the programmers. In constrast, machine learning systems use categories of general algorithms , e.g. neural networks to figure out the relevant mapping on their own, typically by being fed very large data sets of examples. By using these machine learning methods bring the growth in total data and data processing resources, machines have made impressive gains in perception and cognition, two essential skills for most types of human work.

Nowadays, an increasing number of companies have responded to these high technological opportunities to be applied to manufacturing function aspect, such as Google now describes its focus on " AI first", when Microsoft's CEO says (AI) is the " ultimate breakthrough" in technology. Their optimism about (AI) is not just cheap talk. They are making heavy investments to apply (AI) technology in manufacturing function aspect. The possibility is that the gains of (AI) manufacturing function new technologies are already attainable to different kinds of manufacturing industries. Assuming the (AI) robotic manufacturing worker technologies are at least partially rivalrous. Their effect on averge productivity growth is modest overall, and is virtually not essential need fo median worker. For instance, two of the most profitable uses of (AI) for targeting and pricing online ads. and for automated trading of financial instruments, both applications with many zero-sum aspects.

Hence, I predict that future one day will occur many low skillful level workers lose their manufacturing jobs in factories, due to many manufacturing firms choose to apply (AI) robotic machines to replace human labor workers to help them to manufacture any products in order to achieve increasing productivity growth and reducing manufacturing labor number and wages and raising revenue aims. It is really a good reason to be optimistic about the future productivity growth potential of new technologies, such as (AI) robotic machine to be replaced to the traditional slow speed and low efficient productivity and high cost manufacturing method or technique to any factories.

In conclusion, due to manufacturers expect to raise productivity growth aim. It has two main sources of the delay between recognition of a new technology, such as (AI) robotic machine's potential and its measurable effects. One is that it takes time to build the stock in the new technology to a size sufficient enough to have an aggregate effect. The other is that complementary investments are necessary to obtain the full benefit of the new technology, such as (AI) robotic manufacturing technology and it takes time to discover and develop these complements and to implement them. When, the fundamental importance of the core invention and its potential for society might be clearly recognizable at the outset, the myriad necessary co-invention, obstacles and adjustment needed along the way award discovery over time if future one day had another kind new manufacturing technology which can replace (AI) robotic manufacturing method to be better. Hence, it explains that futuer there are many manufacturing industries choose to apply (AI) robotic machines to replace human workers in factory manufacturing environments in order to achieve the raising of productivity growth in efficient way aim more easily.

FOUR

How Robots Improve Organizational Performance

Human Behavioral network job brings social economic benefits

What does human network job mean ? Why may human network job be popular? Why human network job behavior may influence economy ?

Nowadays internet is popular to use. We can apply internet to find data , search any new things, even earn money. Why does internet may become huma network job source. For example, e-publish may be one kind of new human network job. Any authors may apply internet

channel to help them to sell electronic or paper books from e-publisher web store. They may apply facebook, you tub etc. any online

channel to promote themselves new books to let new readers to know whether when they may buy themselves favourable new topic books to read from electronic publisher web store.

Thus, future electronic publisher industry may help any authors to build internet network platform to help them to sell and promote ot advertise their any one new electronic or paper book topic to let global any one reader to choose to buy their any new topic books from electronic publisher web store easily and conveniently. However, it implies that electronic network platform author may be one kind of future new human network job in our societies.

How electronic network platform author job may bring economy benefit in macro economy view? A person can have few friends, contacts and still be very influential if these few
friends and contacts are themselves highly influential, e.g. one author must not need to know any one reader in global society. When they like to choose any electronic books from electronic internet network platform. They may become the author's any one topic book buyer, when they feel the author's any one topic book is fun and attract they make decision to buth the strange author whose the topic book from electronic book publisher's platform web store conventiently in short time. Although, they are strangers, they do not know themselves , but the reader can understand what it way that made Google from writing platofrm to create new creative mind and typing network job method to replace traditional hand writing book method for global authors. It will be one kind of new human network writing job.

Hence, global any one reader can apply an innovative search engine , such as google.com to find whether whom author personal new topic books are value to read from internet.
Then, the electroniuc publisher's web store may be new book store platform sale network to help the author to sell many electronic or paper books from electronic network platform
in short time. So, internet may be future new network plaform to help global any one author to create network writing job absolutely. Furthermore, internet may be popular social media
to help any one author to build goold relationship between his/her readers. It is one kind of new network, human network job. New

authors do not need to buy many paper books to prepare to put in any one book shop warehouse. Their every book can print on demand to reduce out of book stock in any one book shop. They may choose to sell either electronic books or paper books both from any one book publisher web store. So, electronic network platform may be one kind of good writing channel to help human authors to create income and it can also help authors to bring new creative mind and new topic fun content books to let readers to know and buy to read from electronic publisher network platform.

Why does human behavior may be one kind of new human network job to bring global economic advantages. ALthough, it may be free income or without inocme, but the person does the network behavior, his/her behavior may be bring advantages to influence many other people's health. For this case, when a worker in a coffee shop in an airport gets a vaccination aganinst the flu, it does not only helps him or her stay healthy, but also helps the many travellers who might otherwise have been inflected if that workers caught the flu. So, the externality , the result implies the vaccination of even a part of a community conveys benefits to the whole community. For example, governments pay special attention to the vaccinations of school children, teachers, health mothers, and the elderly, categories of people particularly susceptible not only to catching, but also to transmitting a disease.

It is not accidential that governments are heavily involved with vaccination . When there are externalities, free market, fail to persuade individual incentives with society's

their the worker's decision of whether to get a vaccine ends up attracting whether other people get sick. The workers might not fully take all these other people's potential suffering into account when making her or his vaccination decision.

As Stanford University does many suggestions, understand this and tries to help them make the right decisions and so providers free flu vaccines for its staff and students.

Small pockets of unvaccinated individuals can allow a disease to gain a spread more widely well-being. For example, parent weighing the costs and benefits of a vaccine for their child is not always thinking of the consequences of that vaccination to other people. THese are markets in which subsidizing or regulating behavior can make everyone better off. Because the reason for requiring that a child be vaccinated before enrolling in school is not just to protect that child, because each child's vaccination affects others via potential contagions.

Robots take our jobs behavioral and economy influences

Robot job behavior brings economy influences

If one day robots can replace human to do simple, even complex jobs. They will bring what influences to our global societial economy.The popular economic refrain declares that the
global middle class is dying and robots will soon take our jobs, e.g. shopping center customer service jobs, library service jobs, cinema ticket sale jobs, restaurant kitchen cooker jobs,
even, bus drivers, taxi drivers etc. public transport driving jobs, accountant, doctors etc. professional jobs. Whether it is beautiful or petty matter if our future societies have many human jobs can be replaced to do from robots. Businessman must may reduce to employ employees and reduce to pay salary or wage, when robots can be replaced to do their employees tasks. But, societies must bring unemploycment rate rises , due to societies will have many people loss jobs when their employers choose to buy robots to serve their clients or do any office tasks or customer service or cleaning etc. tasks.

In micro economy view, employers may save money in long term, but in macro economy view, it will cause unemployment ratio rises , even crime rate rises when there are many people lose
jobs in societies. These models of doom, though, fail to account for the hundreds of businesses riding the waves of change in their industries when robots may be invented to replace human to do many simple , even complex tasks in our future societies.

WE may image that one small factory needs to manufacture fishes canes to sell to supermarket, the small , cheaper stuff and higher margin parts of the fishes manufacture industry. Before, this factory needs to employe many human factory workers need to help every fresh customer makeing the perfect fishing gear, designed for performance, durability, and cost in order to achieve to manufacture every fish cane in whole fished processing manufacturing stages. Every worker needs to spend about 15 to twenty minutes to finish every fish cane , till to delivery to any supermarket to sell. If this fish canes manufacturing factory can apply manufacturing robots to help them to finish any one working tasks , every robot can only spend five minutes to finish whole fresh fish cane manufacturing process. Thus, every robot can

help this factory save 10 to 15 minutes time to finsh every fish cane manufacturing process. IN fact, time is money, because when every robot can help this factory to reduce 10 to 15 minutes time to compare human worker. Then, this factory can finish about 20 fish canes in one hour if it can use robot to help it to manufacture fish canes. Otherwise, if this factory still use human workers to help it to manufacture fish canes, then it can finsh about 3 to 4 fish canes in one hour. SO, the manufacturing efficiency ensures that robots must help this fish manufacturing factory to raise fish canes number more than human workers. So, in robotic behavioral economy view, manufacturing robots must help this fish canes manufacturing factory to raise fish canes manufacturing number and deliver increasing number to supermarkets to prepare to sell every day. Robots can help this fish canes manufacturing factory bring manufacturing time saving, rising manufacturing efficiency, improving performance and reducing wages expenditure long time advantages in micro economy view. However, manufacturing robots can also bring disadvanages to society, e.g. increasing unemployment ratio, increasing crime rate,

this factory workers will lose jobs and income, they need earn social welfare from government and increasing government finance pressure in short time, even long time in macro economic view.

Stanford University graduate program in economics, Scott lecturer explained that "in demand and supply economic theory for robots supply and demand case, robots supply number increasing may influence human workers demand number decrease. It sometimes calls " the efficient frontier".

No specific human beings were mentioned in any of economics classes. As robots supply and demand in market case, They (robots) may be purely theoretical " agents" who reached to the most reasonable sale prices in order to persuade any one businessman buyer to make manufacturing robot buying decision whether robots can help him / her to bring how much saving time , saving money, saving cost, improving performance, efficiency economic benefit before he/she plans to reduce workers number when he/she decides to apply robots to replace human workers in his/her factory or office or any service department, e.g. cinema ticket sale service, shopping center customer service, shopping center cleaning , supermarket customer service etc. service or sale tasks. When robots can replace human to do any one of these tasks in any organizations. So, robots may be human worker agents who reached to prices the way robots would react to a software command. There was nothing that explained why some people thrived and others did n't or why truly brilliant, hardworking people could fail when much lazier folks succeeded." Having been admitted to the Stanford University graduate program in economics, Scott lecturer hoped to get his answers there.

How robots influence our future social changing? Using the right technology can be a boon to your business in this economy. For internet example, it is easier than ever to find well-matched customers all around the world, to stay in contact with them, and to more quickly design the products they want. If you focus solely on being cutting -edge, though you risk letting the technology take over what should be very robust relationships with your customers , employees, and colleagues. IN nowaddays society, technoligical advances and cutomation, personal relationships in business are more crucial than ever. I mean that robots can not replace human to serve clients to let them to feel more comfortable and passion more easily. For shoe shop case example, if the shoe shop apply one robot to serve its clients to replace human shoe salesperson to serve its shoe customers. Robots ensure that they can not persuade every shoe potential buyer to make shoe buying decision more easily when robots need to contact every shoe potential buyer. The reason is simple, because robots can not touch any one shoe buyer individual emotion very easier.

If the shoe buyer needs the robots to help him/her to choose any right shoe styles when he/she can not feel himself / herself can make the most right shoe style choice decision. The robots can not replace human shoe salesperson to make shoe style choice judgement more easily. They must need longer time to analyze whether which shoe style may be the most suitable to the shoe buyer. Otherwise, human shoe salesperson may attempt to make the most right shoe style choice decision to help any one shoe buyer to chooce the most right style shoe because he/she owns shoe style sale experience, shoe style knowledge, the most important reason is that they can feel every shoe customer individual emotion to touch whether he/she will feel comfortable or happy when they attempt to help every shoe customer to seek the most right shoe style in every shoe customer whole shoe searching processing. Othwerwise, serving robots are only one machine, they can not touch or feel every shoe customer individual emotion whether he/she feel comfortable or unhappy or happy when they need to contact them in whole shoe searching processing. Hence, I believe that some tasks robots can

not repalce human staff to do very easily. Otherwise, robots may bring disadvanatges to let any one businessman to loss his/her customers, due to robots can not touch every customer

emotion to compare human staff in service tasks more easily. Robots serving customer behaviors may cause money lose and customers number lose to the shop in micro economic view.

Intellectual human economic behaviors

What does intellectual human economic behaviors mean ? I believe that when we choose or decide to do intellectual behaviors, then our societies will be influenced to bring economic growth in consequence.I shall attempt to indicate pollution case to explain how and why eithet our intellectual or foolish behaviors may bring economic growth or recession in consequence as below:

On one hand, for air pollution social case aspect example, if we only consider to buy cars to drive for working aimr or holiday leisure aim. Then, our societies air will be polluted. Our health will be influenced to bad. Our car driving behaviors may cause global environment air pollution serously. In long tiem, global air pollution will bring our bodies health to be bad. Although, ourselves car driving behaviors may bring our driving travelling leisure enjoyment and comfortable feeling in short time, also we so not need to pay public transport fare often, but we need to compensate ourselves health economic intangible loss due to air pollution , when cars number increases, dirty air will cause ouselves health to become bad.

In the result, we will need to pay more medical expenditure when we are old age, due to ourselves bodies will become bad, due to we breathe global dirty air every day, due to ourselves cars pollute air in long time, e.g. 10 to 20 years, even 30 more without limited air pollution environment. So, driving cars behavior may be one kind of human foolish behavior and our foolish behavior may bring ourselves future long time medical expenditure absolutely.

One the other hand, water pollution social aspect, if we often keep much rubblish to pollute sea, oil exploration porcessing pollute ocean , ships gas pollute ocaen, then fishes will eat polluted food and drive dirty water, due to global ocean is polluted.

In fact, because human only to conside how to buy boats to carry on leisure enjoyment activities, or catch cruises to travel on the sea. Also, oil manufacturers only consider researching anywhere to find new oil exploration places to manufacture oil product, when their oil exploration processes pollute ocarn . Consequently, global fishes drink polluted warer or eat polluted food. They will have poison. SO, human will have high chance to eat poison polluted fishes, due to fishes are poison or are polluted.

So, human is doing foolish activities, we only hope to find oil exploration places to pollute ocean or we only spend money to buy ticket to catch ships to travel anywhere in global ocean. All of these human foolish behaviors will bring pollution to global ocean. On consequently, we will need to compensate to eat polluted or dirty or poision fishes, ourselves bodies health will be bad. In long time, we need have high chance to pay medical expenditure when we are old. So, pollution case may be one good example to explain how and why human foolish behavior may influence ourselves future need to compensate serious medical loss.

All of these human foolish behavior will bring pollution to global ocean. On consequently, we will need to compensate to eat polluted or dirty or poison fished , ourselves bodies health will be bad. In long time, we will have high chance to pay medical expenditure, when we are old. So, pollution case may be one good example to explain how and why human ourselves intellectual or foolish behaviors may influence future long time economic loss or economic growth or recession in micro and micro economic view.

On another water pollution aspect hand, if we often keep rubbish to sea, oil exploration processing pollutes ocean and ships' gas pollute ocean, then fishes will eat polluted food and drink dirty water, due to fishes will eat polluted food and drink dirty sea water because the global ocean is polluted seriously.

In fact, because human only consider how to buy boats to carry on any leisure water activities, or catches cruises to travel on the sea. Also, oil manufacturers only consider any where to find oil exploratin places to manufacture oil products from ocean, when their pol exploration processes can plooute ocean. Consequently, global fishes drink polluted water or eat direty food. They will have poison. So, human will have high chance to eat poison fishes.

Otherwise, such as pollutin case, it can infuence inflation or deflation. Consequently, the reason indicates supply and demand theory. If air pollution is serious, then we will consider health issue, global cars demand number may be influenced to reduce, when global cars number demand will reduce, global car prices and supply number will need to change to fall down in order to attract or persuade global car consumers choose to make car purchase decision.

Hence, global car manufacture number and car price will be influenced to reduce, due to global air pollution issue. Consequently, deflation will occur because when the country citizen usually does not spend much extra saving money to buy car expensive goods. Money value will be low. Otherwise, if global cair pollution is not serious, human considers to buy cars to enjoy driving leisure lives. So, global car demand is influenced to increase , also global car price will also influenced to increase.

Consequently, gobal human will choose to buy cars to drive. Due to we accept to spend extra saving to buy expensive car goods. Car sale price and supply may be influenced to rise up. Money value is influenced to reduce. Inflation may be influenced, due to global car consumers number increases, we would not have extra money to spend easily. Car expensive goods expenditure influences our spending habit to avoid to make car purchase decision more easily. So, human intellectual or foolish activities may bring inflation or deflation consequency in possible indirectly in macro economic view.

On conclusion, above pollution case explain that how and why human intellectual or foolish economic behaviors may bring inflation or deflation consequency as wll as economic growth or recession consequency as well as any goods demand and supply increasing or decreasing consequency. It implies that human behavior may have indirect relationship to influence any goods demand and supply number to either increase or decrease result as well as any goods price will be influenced to increase or decrease in micro and macro economic view.

The relationship between social change and human behavior

Why does economic changes may influence human individual behavioral change? I shall attempt to indicate shopping behavior and staying at home behavior to explain their case and effect relationsip as below:

Human behavior can be influenced by economic change or

economic change can be influenced by human behavior? Why does recession may influence consumers reduce shopping desire? In social recession suitation, it is possible that many people lose jobs suddenly, due to businessmen lose many customers. They need to make decision to reduce employees number in order to continue to keep businesses. Consequently, many firms (organizations) their employees may lose jobs. When they have much time, due to lose jobs, they will feel to avoid to spend too much time and money to go to shopping often. Many losing jobs people, they will often stay at homes.

So, they will reduce time to go to shopping, then non essential products won't their preferable choice purchase products. Hence, recession will change many losing jobs people their shopping or consumption desires to avoid to buy non essential products often . Usually when economic boom, many people have jobs to do because consumers number must increase when many people have jobs to do. Then, many people can accept to spend money to buy non essential products often. Many people feel spend time to go to shopping can satisfy their purchase of any kinds of new products useful psychology or desire. So, recession is one good example to explain it can influence many people do not like often to leave homes to go to shopping easily. Many people like to stay at homes, becaue they feel worry about spending too much shopping time when they leave homes. Their staying home time is one good negative shopping behavior example. So, economic change may influence human individual behavior changes , they have direct cause and efect relationship in behavioral economic view.

May human behavior influence economic change? Is it possible that human behavior may bring the country social economic change in macro economic or micro behavioral economic view ? I shall indicate publishing industry example. Do you feel that if there are many students feel learning is very important when they read many books or many of students feel interesting to read or they have reading new books in habit, then it is possible that the country will have many students like to spend time to go to any book shops to choose the books, they feel that they can help they learn new knowledge. Then the country will increase students number, they often spend time to visit any one book shop every week. Their visiting book shops behavior which may become their habits. So, the country will increase students number, they often spend time to visit book shops. Also, it implies that visiting book shops behaviors may be their behavioral habits.

So, when the country has many students often spend time to visit book shops , their visiting book shops behaviors may help any one book shop to raise books sale chance. So, the country's student individual often visiting book shop behaviors, their habitual visiting book shops behaviors must may assist help any one book shop to increase books sale number absolutely.

Consequently, any one book shop , its books sale bumber must be influenced to increase to increase because the country will have many students like or feel need visit book shops habit in order to choose any suitable books to buy to read at home in order to raise themselves learning effort. When the country has many bok shops often have many students visit their book shops, then their books sale number may be influenced to increase. It explain why student individual visiting book shop behavior may help any one book shop sale number increases also.

How human productive behavior may influence economic development

May any country which citizen behavior assist themselves country development? It is one cause and effect economic question. I mean that if the country itself citicen can not concentrate mind or energy to choose to do one kind of industry in order to let themselves country can bring the most benefit, then whether the counry itself economy can bring the most serious economic benefit. I shall attempt to indicate these countries themselves indistry choice to explain whether these countries themselves citizen productive behavior may help themselves countries to achieve the largest economic benefits. I shall indicate as below:

New Zealand farmer individual wine productive behavior

For New Zealand country example, this country concerns itself effort is foucs on farming agricultural aspect. So, this country has many farmers concentrate on farming agricultural aspect. May New Zealanders choose to spend time to produce different kinds of wines, e.g. wine or red grape wine is for the people are eating meat, or they are eating dinner.

When these New Zealanders their behaviors choose to do farming or agriculture to grow and produce different kinds of taste of white or red grape wine drinking products job. Themselves grape agriculture behavior will influence these New Zealanders themselves, they can learn how to improve different kinds of grape wine drinking products in order to achieve every kinds of white or read grape wines taste improving aim during their white or red grape producing process.

Why can New Zealander every individual white or read grape wine producers improve their white or read grape wine taste more easily? In behavioral economic view, it can explain that why any one New Zealander white or read grape wine producer can be encouraged or excited or persuaded to concentrate nervous and energy and effort to learn how to improve their white or red grape wine products easily.

In fact, New Zealand is one agricultural food export country. It has good natural environment resource , e.g. land, seed to provide any one farmer to produce themselves any kinds of agricultrual food products, e.g. fruit, or wine food products. Because New Zealanders know themselves country has enough natural resource . So, in common, many New Zealanders choose to attempt to do farming agricultural jobs in order to export themselves any kinds of fruit or meat or wine products to overseas or sell to domestic in order to earn profit.

So, when these New Zealand farmers number has been increasing every year. This country farmers will feel themsleves competition between this New Zealand farmers themselves are serious due to they may feel New Zealanders choose to do agriculture businesses in order to export themselves different kinds of farming food to

overseas or sell to local to earn profit.
Hence, when many New Zealand farmers feel that farmers number has been increasing every year. They will feel themselves competition is serious. They must need to spend much time and nervous and effort to research what method is the best how to produce the best taste of white or red grape wine products in order to let local or overseas wine buyers to choose to buy his/her producing white or read grpae products to drink.
Hence, in competition psychological view, may influence many New Zealand white or reaad wine producers had been beginning to change their learning behavior on researching what method is the best in order to produce the best quality of taste red or white wine products to sell in order to attract overseas or local white or read grape wine drinkers to choose to buy his/her wine products. Their behavior will focus on learning how to raising or improving white or read grape wine taste method more than only focus on producing a large number white or red grape wine products. They believe wine quality is more important to compare wine producing number. So, New Zealand wine producers themselves wine producers behaviors have been changing on concentrating on researching wine quality method aspect more then wine producing number aspect in behavioral economic view.

America high technological productive behavior

For America example, US is one high technological country, it owns many high technological knowledge talent inventors, e.g. computer science inventors. Hence, US must attract many diferent countries owning high technological computer inventors choose to go to US to develop their computer science profession career. Also, it seems that when many computer science inventors or professions choose to go to US to develop themselves computer science new career. In behavioral economic view, due to their leaving themselves countries choice, which may bring influence themselve country job behaviors need to be changed. They must need to adapt US new live. Because they will forgive their past computer science job. These computer science professionals need to spend time to adapt US new lives.

They " past computer science job behaviors" will need to be changed to their new US any computer employer's new computer science job model.

Because their traditional computer science jobs needed to be forgot in their themselves countries. They will feel their old computer science job knowledge and behavior needed to change in order to let their US any one new of computer company employer feels satisfactory to accept their new working behavior in any one US computer organization.

So, on the other hand, many US computer company employer will feel that they must need time to accept any one new overseas computer science professions their working behaviors, their working attitude daily, because these foreign comouter science professional, their past computer working behaviors and working attitude must be different to US domestic computer science professions.

In behavioral economic view, these overseas computer science professions, their working behaviors and attitude must be needed to change in order to adapt any one US new computer company itself domestic or local computer science professional stafs themselves daily working behaviors and attitude because these overseas and local computer science professionals must need to team work together.

In behavioral economic view, it is only one way that foreign computer science professionals must need to change themselves past country traditiona daily working behaviors and attitude in order to cooperate with these US local computer science professionals in teams more easily.

Consequently, if these foreign compute science professionals can change their past working behaviors and attitude to let any one US local computer science professional feels to cooperate with them easily in short time. Then, the US computer company itself whole computer professional teams themselves efficiencies will be influenced to raised or improved by the changing past working attitude and working behaviors of these foreign computer science professionals. So, in behavioral economic view, only if US any one computer company hopes itself computer teams themselves efficiency can be raised or improved when it decides to employ foreign computer science professionals and US domestic computer science professionals. They need to work in teams together. They must need to let these foreign computer science professionals to know how to change their working behaviors and attitude to let their domestic computer science professionals feel easy to work together. Then, the US computer company itself whole team efficiency must be rasied or improved easily in short time.

- China share market investing behavior

For China share market example, economic development depends on financial market. Because if many Chinese have interest to invest to carry on shares buying and selling activities in orde to learn how to earn shares interest and share profit when the China shareholder can make decision to sell himself/herself shares in the the high price, then he/she can earn money when he/she can sell the China company's shares in the high sale share price position.

If China has many Chinese like to spend time to carry on investing shares activities. Themselves shares buying and selling behaviors will influence China has many companies can increase fund from many Chinese shareholders in order to have enough money to expand or develop themselves businesses in China in long term.

Consequently, when China can have many Chinese like to attempt to carry on buying and selling shares investing behaviors in China share market. Themselves buying and selling shares behaviors can help many Chinese companies have effort to increase enough money or capital in order to continue to do their businesses in long term absolutely. So, it explains why when many Chinese become shareholders , they can assist China will have many companies continue to develop their businesses if many Chinese like to carry on shares buying and selling investing behaviors in long time in China financial investment market nowadays in behavioral economic view.

Why has any individual country have many people invest share behavior which can influence the country's macro consumption desire?

I shall apply shares market buying and selling investment behavior to explaiin why shares investment behavior which may impact the country's overal consumption desire as below:

In behavioral economic view, I assume that when the coutry has many people have interest to attempt to carry on shares buying and selling investment behavior, then their frequent shares buying and selling behaviors which may bring negactive consumption desire or shopping desire of these shares investors their consumer behavior.

The reason is simple, when the country has many share buyers number suddenly been increasing rapidly. Consequently, these large group share investors must need to spend much time to research any kinds of company shares variations, whether when their share prices will rise up of fall down in order to achieve buying the company's shares in the lowest price and selling the company's shares in the highest price level in order to earn profit.

Basic on this reason, they must need to spend much extra time to research share prices changing behavior every day, e.g. one working person will wait to leave his/her job, after he/she can spend time to gather data to research the day's share price changing behavior after dinner. So, the working person's right time may be his/her share price market research behavior. Before he/she may spend his/her night time to go to shopping after dinner, but nowadays, he/she will fogive to do his/her shopping behavior before dinner or after dinner at hight sometime. He/she will make decision to spend much night time to turn on computer to click on share market website to research his/her share purchase choice to investigate whether his/her share price whether it rises up or falls down at the moment in order to make his/her share buying or selling decision at ever night time.

I mean the when the country has many people are share investors, their shares investment behavioral spenging time which will influence many shops lose customers at might often because the country will have many people feel need to spend night time to turn on computer or watch television to investigate share price variation. So, the country will have many people / share investors choose to stay at home in order to carry on share price variation investigation behavior, they need to listen share market update news from radios or watch the share market update news from computer or TV at home every night. Consequenly, they must reduce times to leave themselves homes at night. So, their shopping behavior also will be reduced. Because these share investors feel need to spend time to investigate share price variation news at homes which can bring economic benefits (high opportunity benefits) when they choose to forgive to leave homes to go to shopping times (opportunity cost) every night.

On conclusion, it seems that when the country has many people are share investors, then their share price investigating behavior may bring negative shopping emotion at night. Consequently, the country's any one shop may lose many customers from this share investor consumer group in behavioral economic view. Hence, when the country's share investors number had been increasing rapidly, it will influence any shops lose many customers from this share investing customer group at night frequenly in short time, even long time in behavioral economic view, because their shopping desires or shopping emotion will be brought negative feeling when they make decisions to spend much time to listen radios or watch TV or computers share price update nes at night. Hence, share market will bring negative impact to influence consumer shopping desire or negative shopping emotion in behavioral economic view.

Can technology influence human shopping behavioral change?

Nowadays, technological development has reached mature stage, whether technological mature stage may bring positive or negative shopping emotion influence to global consumers. I shall aplly internet inventin or ecommerce shopping channel tool to explain whether internet technology can bring postive or negative influence to global consumer behavior in behavioral economic view.

Internet is a good technological tool, it brings e-commerce business chance. In fact, commonly, global has have many businessmen choose to use internet channel to carry on their products transactions between global online-buyers and their electronic websites. So, global many shoppers had begun to feel online shopping is more convenient to compare visiting shops shopping. Their shopping behaviors have been changed from internet technological tool. Global has many shoppers choose to buy any products from any overseas or local businessmen their web stores. They only need to spend time to find any businessmen their webstores to choose the most suitable products to pay visa to buy from their webstores. at homes. So, in general, global had have may shoppers had changed their shopping behaviors from visiting shops to visiting webstores at homes often.

So, it seems that internet technological tool had influenced global many shops disappear, but internet webstores will be replaced their actual shops on streets. Some of businessmen either they choose webstores to replace shops or choose websotes and shops both or still keep shops only. Hence, internet tool influences global businessmen have three kinds of products sale channels to let globa local and overseas consumers to choose how to buy their products.

However, in fact, many of global shoppers, youngers and olders had begun to accept to buy any products from webstores. They feel to spend time to leave homes to visit shops , their shopping behaviors will be wasted time to not essential part to their daily lives. Hence, since internet technological invention, it had changed many consumers their traditional visiting shops shopping habit to change to buying products from webstores channel.

However, on the one hand, internet creates webstores ecommerce shopping channel to let global many consumers do not need to leave homes to go to shopping. It brings negative visiting shops shopping emotion to global general consumers nowadays. But on the other hand, it also brings positive visiting internet webstores shopping emotion to global general consumer nowadays. So, it seems that global many consumers feel that they often do not need to spend much time to go out shopping. Many global consumers feel convenient and enjoy to choose any products to buy from different internet webstores, when the online buyer chooses the most suitable product, he she only needs to pay visa card to buy the product from the online seller's webstore conveniently at home.

Hence, online shopping can bring economic benefit to online buyers, e.g. avoiding walking time or spending transport fare to visit the shop to go to shopping, shortening or reducing shopping time to do another important matter.

On conclusion, global many consumers began feel online shopping can bring more economic benefits on shortening shopping time, avoiding transport fare spending aspect. So, online shopping will be popular shopping behavior for future long time. It may encourage global many shoppers can make rapid shopping decision in short time in order to carry on any products buying transaction to global any one online shopper in short time easily in behavioral economic view. So, global many businessmen had begun to build themselves one attraction webstore in order to persuade different countries consumers to choose to click themselves webstores from internet channel to buy any kinds of products in short time easily.

So, internet technology had changed consumers traditional shopping behaviors to build positive online shopping emotion as well as raise online sellers' any products sale chance easily in behavioral economic view.

Why and how human behavior may influence the country's economic growth or recession?

When one country has many people choose to do the same matter for one period, whether their behavior may influence the country's pvera; economic growth or recession . I shall attempt to indicate cases toexplain their relationship as below:

For flowing rubblish behavioral case example, do you feel that when the country has many people often flow rubblish on the streets, instead of their flowing rubblish behavior may bring streets dirty? But, their flowing rubblish behavior may explain that this country has people may have enough money to buy food to ear, or enough cloths to wear, enough bottles of water to drink, even they may have enough money to buy new television, radio, refrigeraters , washing machines, desktops or laptops electronic home products from old to new to use in order to satisfy their living needs. So, when they flow old electronic home products, their flowing old home electronic products behaviors may seem that they have enough money to buy other new home electronic products to replace old home electronic products to use at homes.

However, it seems thaat this country ought have many people have jobs to do. So, many of them, they can easy to make purchase decison to flow any old home electronic products and buy any new home electronic products to use . Because this country has many people have jobs to do. So, they can often not use old home electonic products to become rubblishs to flow on streets after they had bought any kinds of new home electronic homes.

In fact, it also implies that this country's economy grows rapidly. So, many businesses can glow up rapdly. When they expanded their businesses, they must need to increase employees number in order to let they help themselves to raise productivity or serve their clients absolutely. So, when the country has many businesses can grow up, it seems that its economy must be better or it is improved to compare past. Due to many different kinds of home electronic products had been often bought to use by this country people in this period. So, this country's any streets can be observed that expensive electronic home products were flowed on streets anywhere. then, this country will have many electronic home products sellers can sell their home electronic products very easily. When this country has many people can find any kinds of jobs to do easily. So, due to unemploymen rate had been decreasing.

In behavioral economic view, as this many electronic home products rubblish country case, we can observe this country may have many people have jobs to do. So, consumption number has been increased long time. So, cheap food, or expensive home electronic products may be rubblish on any streets. This country's people , their flowing rubblish behaviors may be explained that many of people have enough jobs to do, so they have ability to buy any good taste food to eat or buy any kinds of expensive electronic home products to use. So, this country's economy may be improved for this long period. So, in behavioral economic view, when this country can have many electronic home products rubblishs are flowed on anywherer in streets frequently. It seems that this country will have many people have jobs to do, so it causes they often change old home electronic products or replaced them easily, when they have enough income to spend to buy any kinds of new home electronic products to use at homes easily. Moreover, their flowing old electronic home products behaviors also indicate that this country has many people their salaries may be increased in possible from their emplyers. When this country can have many different kinds of home electornic products are sold. It means that this country's electronic home products needs or demand had been increasing, due to many people have jobs to do and income increases to excite their living of needs also improve. Consequently, this country may seem have better economic improvement. We can observe from this country's electronic home products rubblish increasing income in theis period.

On conclusion, this country ought experience economic growth at this period. So, " flowing expensive electronic home rubblish increasing number " may seem that this country's economic growth is rapidly in this period, due to many people have jobs to do as well as salaries increase in this period.

Technology how impacts human behavior changing?

Technology how influences human behavior to bring changing? For example, online share purchase and sale transaction from smart phone brings share investor can do share buying or selling transation in any where and any time conveniently, non manual driving auto vehicle, bring car owner feels comfortable and spends free time to do other matter, e.g. reading, listening mucis in himself or herself car freely. electrical energy vehicle can help car owner to reduce air polluton and it can brings the drivers do not feel drive long time in any journeys in order to avoid air pollution for environmental protection responsible car drivers in our societies. Thus, they will drive long time in any journeys when they can drive electronic energy cars to replace oil energy cars.

However, online technology can also bring consumers can choose to stay at homes to buy any things from seller individual online webstore conveniently. Such as online technology can bring shoppers do not need to spend much time to visit shops to buy any things. They can choose any kinds of products from any online sellers individual online webstores conveniently at homes. Online technology excite busy consumers can make purchase decision easily as well as it can help online sellers sell any kinds of products from internet easily.

In behavioral economic view, technology can change human behavior to be improved, it can let human feels comfortable, more free time ro use, rapid making any decisions, such as apply smart phones to make share purchase or sale transaction decision, online shopping decision, even travelling any where decision in short time, when the traveller finds the most cheap hotel accommodation room price and air ticket price frm any travel agent online tourism webstore, then the potential travel customer can follow the online hotel accommodation price and air ticket price data to make decision when to buy the air ticket from the airline travel agent or make decision when to prebook which hotel accommodation room to go to the country to travel from online travel agent tourism webstores. So, technology can encourage global any country travelers to make anywhere to trvel rapidly. If the traveler can find the country's general hotel rooms and airline tickets prices had been decreasing more sightly. The traveler may make travel decision to choose the country to travel in short time, then he/she can prebook the country;s any hotel room and airline ticket to pay by visa fraom the country's any hotel and airline travel agent webstores., before one week, even one month or more easily. Hence, online technology can also encourage traveler individual frequent travel times to be increased, due to global travelers can find any hotel rooms and airline tickets prices from internet conveniently at homes. They do not need to spend time to visit any airline travel agent to enquire travel choice country's hotel rooms prices and airline ticket prices. They can compare global travel of countries choices ' all hotels rooms and airline agents air tickets prices to make prebook airline seat and hotel room decision before one week, one month even six months early.

On conclusion, online technology can encourage global travelers can make travelling any where and when traveling time desicions easily. It can excite tourism industry develops in long time. Also, such as electricity cars invention can encourage environment protection car owners do car purchase decision easily, because they can choose to drive electronic energy cars to replace oil energy cars in order to avoid air pollution occurs easily. So, electronic cars can increase electronic car purchasrs number, due to many of environmental protection attitude of car owners can choose to drive electricity cars to bring air cleans, even non -manual driving cars can encourage lazy driving and free time driving car owners to choose to buy non-manual (artificial intelligent) cars to drive , because they can spend much free time to read, listen music or do any matters in themselves cars, they do not need to drive cars, robotic (AI) auto driving machine is such one non-manual driver to help them to drive themselves cars confidently. So, non-manual driving cars can attract lazy and enjoying free time driving car owners to choose to buy to replace traditional manual cars to drive easily. Moreover, online share transaction can help any share investors to make share buying and selling decision in short time easily. When they can apply smart phones technological tool to carry on share buying and selling activities easily. They can observe any share rising or falling price suitation from smart phones in any where any any time easily. So, smart phone technology can help global any shareholders to make share purchase and sale transaction easily. So, technology can encourage human makes decision in short time rapidly.

How and why employees behaviors may influence economy development?

In behavioral economy view,I believe the country's any organizational employees behavior may bring indirect relationship to influence the country's long term economic development. I shall indicate past manufacture industry social development period to explain their relationship. For many countries' past business activities had belonged to manufacturing industry, such as US, UK past before 1980 year, it focused on steel manufacturing and steel manufacturing related machine products. So, US, Uk developed countries manufacturing industries may be past main country's economic income sources. I assume US , UK past had one million number different kinds of industries. They ought had about seven houndred thousand number organizational businesses were belonged to manufactured industry. They may include:

Steel manufacturing and steel related machine manufacturing, e.g. vehicle manufacturing, home appliances, e.g. washing machine, television, radio, refrigerate cooler, heater, air condition etc. different kinds of different kinds of steel -related manufacturing machine, they were manufactured from US, UK steel machine manufacturers. So, US, Uk the other three hundred thousand number industry may be general service industry, e.g. hotel service, restaurent, cinema, public transport service, tourism lesiure , wine bar, supermarket etc. different kinds of non-manufacturing industries business organizations were operated in UK, US past before 1980 year.

So, in UK, US developed countries industry development history, they ought have high percentage of businesses belonged to steel related manufacturing machine and steel products. Also, in the past before 1980 year, US, Uk business employers , they employed many workers are manufacturing workers. They needed to spend long time to work in factories. They were skillful workers, and they are trained to manufacturing cars, washing machine, television, heater, etc. even steel itself different kinds of steel related products to prepare to deliver to their shops to sell to US, Uk local or overseas clients.

So, I believe that past UK, US ought employ many employees, they belonged to skillful manufacturing workers, manufacture increasing steel machine or steel related machine number of products rapidly daily. So, if UK, US had had many of these manufacturing factories owned high skillful workers, then their manufacturing steel-related machine or steel both kinds of products number must be influenced to raise rapidly. Consequently, their steel machine manufacturing products would been exported to overseas or would been sold to local both markets , they may be influenced to raise sale number. They (these manufacturing workers) needed to be trained to know how to manufactur these different kinds of machine products in the efficient teams and they ought to be trained to raise their efficiencies in order to shorten time to manufacturing many kinds of steel related manufacturing machine or steel itself products rapidly. So , if their efficiencies and manufacturing performance was improved, these US, UK any one manufacturing worker and their teams ought achieve raising productivities significantly.

Hence, when past UK, US manufacturing industry development period, if these two countries‘ any manufacturing factories could have many manufacturing workers could be trained to be skillful and proficient manufacturing workers. Then, in past every day to these factories workers, they ought help their steel or steel related manufacturing employers to raise any kinds of machine or steel products number in every team. So, when past in the manufacturing industry development, US, UK could have many factories’ manufacturing workers themselves steel or steel related machine products manufacturing skill could be trained to to improve to any kinds of these machine or steel manufacuring products quality as well as their products number could be influenced to raise by themselves skillful improvement significantly every day.

Then, what would be influenced to occur to past UK, US

manufacturing industry period? In behavioral economic view, when these two manufacturing industry developed countries, such as UK, US , if they had many factories workers can be trained to improve their skill in order to achieve any kinds of steel or steel-related machine products quality could be improved as well as products manufacturing number could be also increased absolutely. In consequence, past UK and US both countries ought increase themselves any kinds of steel and steel related machine products number to be supplied to themselves local shops to let local clients to choose any one kind of machine manufacturing products to buy easily as well as they could also export to supply overseas any countries to buy their different kinds of steel or steel related machine products to let overseas steel or steel related manufacturing machine product buyers, they can have many of these different kinds of these steel or steel-related different kinds of manufacturing machine from UK and UK these both countries easily to compare other countries.

On conclusion, I believe that past US, and UK macro manufacturing industry income GDP would increase significantly. So, they would have good economic growth performance because when many of these manufacturing workers themselves manufacturing effort could be improved. So, it explained when employees manufacturing abilities can influence economic growth indirectly.

Robots invention whether they can help organizations to raise efficiencies or inefficiencies?

In behavioral economic view, in any organizations, when the organization hopes its worker teams can raise efficiencies , the organization may choose to increase more workers number and/or it can provide training to improve these workets themselves skills in order to raise their efficiencies. For one warehouse example, when the warehouse increases many goods , they are needed to delivered these goods from the shelves to the delivering destination locations. If this warehouse supervisors feel these workers themselves goods delivery speeds are slow, which is possible due to this warehouse's workers number is not enough. So, this warehouse supervisor ought increase workers number in order to increase their goods delivery speed in order to deliver goods from the shelves to every indicated goods delivery destination in order to let any one lorry driver can transport the right kinds of goods and ensure the accurate goods number to transport to any one client home rapidly.

However, if this warehouse supervisor planed to buy several warehouse goods delivery robots to assist these warehouse workers to find the right kinds of goods from shelves and then deliver to the right destination location in the warehouse. So, these warehouse orkers can concentrate on counting the accurate goods number and ensuring the right kinds of goods in order to prepare to let lorry drivers to transport these goods to these goods of buyers themselvers homes rapidly. Consequently, in the first step, robots can concentrate on finding th right goods from shelves and delivers them to the right goods transportation of location destination. Then, in the second step, these warehouse workers can concentrate on counting the accurate goods number and ensuring the right kinds of goods in order to prepare to put them to the lorry. Consequently, when warehouse robots and warehouse workers can cooperate to work together, the most important, robots, can deal on finding the right kinds of goods and deal on delivering the accurate number of goods of job duty as well as these warehouse workers can only concentrte on counting the right kinds of goods number in order to avoid it has none any mistake of wrong kinds of goods and inaccurate goods of delivery number to be transported to the lorry and to deliver to any one buyer's home.

So, it seems that warehouse robots ought help any one warehouse worker to raise himself efficiency and avoid goods delivery of mistake occurrence easily as well as their help to warehouse workers that can let any one goods buyer feels their goods can be delivered to their homes rapidly. Moreover, warehouse robots can also help these warehouse workers to raise efficiencies because warehouse robots can help them to shorten goods delivery time between any one shelf and any one goods delivery destination of location in the warehuse because robots may help them to find the right kinds of goods from the right shelf in the short time. So, any one worker does not need to spend long time to seek anywhere is the right shelf location for the kind of goods when the kind of goods are needed to deliver to the buyer's home from lorry. Warehouse robots can help them to do this aspect of " finding the goods from the right shelf in short time job duty". So, any one warehouse worker only needed tospend less time to do the counting of any right kind of goods number and ensuring the right kind of goods job duty. Consequently, this warehouse 's any one worker, his any one kind of goods delivery time may be reduced, because robots' assistance and they may have more confidence to avoid mistake to deliver the wrong number of goods and/or the wrong kind of goods to any one goods buyer's home.

On conclusion, it seems that warehouse robots ought may help any one warehouse worker to raise efficiency for any one team in the warehouse as well as the warehouse any one supervisor does not need to spend much time to observe any one worker individual performance for " goods delivery job duty aspect" because their goods delivery job duty that had been replaced to do by these several warehouse robots. Robots can achieve the more accurate of right kinds of goods and the right number of goods delviery job performance to compare any one of human warehouse worker themselves right kinds of goods of delivery and right number of goods of delivery job performance. So, when robots can participate to cooperate with this warehouse's any one worker to do their goods of delivery job duty in this warehouse every day. Then, robots can raies any one of supervisor individual confidence in order to let they do not need to spend time to observe any one of worker individual whose goods of delivery job performane. They can concentrate on supervising any one worker whose goods transport to lorry in the final step in order to avoid to deliver wrong goods number and / or wrong kind of goods to any one goods buyer's home every day. Consequently, this warehouse's overall teams of their delviery of goods performance many be improved by robotss' participatin to goods of delivery task as well as this warehouse's oveall teams themselves efficiencies may be influenced to raise by robots' goods of delivery task participation.

Why social behavior may influence organizational strategy needs to be changed ?
Why any organizations need to know whether nowadays social behaivor how has been changing in order to implement the kind of the most right strategy to achieve the profit aim pursue in possible. I shall indicate nowadays ecommerce or online, customer shopping behavior to explain above question concerns they ought have close relationship between social behavior and organizational strategic choice or organizational behavioral changing need.
On nowadays ecommerce business, or online shopping model, this kind of shopping model in global many young and old age consumers like to apply internet tool to choose any country sellers website stores in order to stay at home to buy any kinds of products from themselves webstores in global societies.
In fact, online shopping model had been popular for long time above to twenty years. Most of global sellers will make decision to design themselves webstores in order to attract global many online buyers to choose to buy their products from themselves webstores. So, it seems that social consumers purchase behaviors had been changed to online shopping from internet invention.
Hence, social consumers purchase behavioral changes may influence any organizations' strategies need to be changed from visiting shops purchase strategy model to online purchase strategy model, if the seller still concentrate on concentrate on considerate how to design itelf , but neglects to considerate how to design itself webstore, e.g. how to design attract product photos to put on itself webstore, how to arrange sale price information location to be putted on webstore and visa card payment location on itself webstore in order to let any one online buyer can feel very easier to buy itself any kinds of products from itself webstore. Then, its potential online buyers will be influenced to increase number when they can find this online seller itself any kinds of products photes

and every kinds of product sale price information and visa card payment channel locations easily from itself webstore.

So, it implies that nowadays any one seller ought need to design one webstore to let any one online overseas and domestic consumers can have chance to click itself webstore to choose any one kind of product to buy conveniently when he/she does not hope to leave him/her home to go to shop, because nowadays social shopping behaviors had been influenced to change when internet invention, them it gives another online purchase method to replace visiting shops purchase method to global any one buyer in nowadays societies.

So, if nowadays any one seller still concentrate on how to design itself shop display in order to put any kinds of product on shelf in order to let any one visiting shop customer to find the kind of product to buy, but it neglects to change to choose to pursue another new technological shopping method, such as webstore purchase method in order to implement effective strategy to design the most right webstore as well as in order to attract global overseas and local consumers to find itself webstore easily from website and find its any one kind of product phots and sale price and visa card payment button in order to choose to buy itself any kinds of products in the short time. Consequently I believe that the seller will lose many customers from overseas and local when its other same or similar product sellers choose to design themselves webstores in order to let global any one product buyer can buy themselves any one kind of product when they can pay visa card to buy their products from them webstores conveniently when they stay at home habitly. Then, the seller will lose many global potential customers in long time.

On conclusion, in behavioral economic view, any consumer behavioral social changing, which will influence any in order to avoid customers number loses significantly . In future time, organizations need to make rapid decision in order to implement the most reasonable and the most useful strategy in order to avoid global potential customers number reduces or lose them in long time. So, social behavioral changing environment ought influence any global organizations need to decide how to change themselves strategies in order to avoid customers loses significantly in future time.

How and why human behavior may influence economic growth or recession?

May ourselves daily behaviors influence our global societial continue economic growth or recession? Do they have cause and effect close relationship between human behaviors and global economic growth or recession? I shall apply behavioral economic theory to analyze and explain whether ourselves daily behaviors and our global societial economic growth or recession which have close cause and effect relationship as below:

Every country itself economic development must depend on any business activities, otherwise, any kinds of business activities must need ourselves business activities or behaviors in order to achieve any business activities as well as achieve the country's overall economic development in macro view.

However, any country's overall business activites or behaviors which must depend on any kinds of individual businessmen, themselves employees daily working behavior or activity or performance in order to help them to attract or increase many clients number to acieve " earning profit" aim. So, it seems that any individual business, itself overall every department individual working behavior is one main factor to influence the company's overall business performance.

For agricultural fruit and meat food farming industry example, such as New Zealand is a farming main target industry country. It had had many New Zealanders were daily themselves own farming businesses for many years. Their farming businesses include growing fruit, sheep, cow, pig pork, meat etc. food sale business. If the New Zealand farmer owned a large size farming land, then he will choose either growing fruit or feeding sheeps, pigs, cows to be meat to to transport to New Zealand supermarkets to help them to sell to their farmers meet to New Zealanders in order to earn profit. Thus, if the New Zealand farmer owned large size of farming lands, then he needs to employ many farming employees (farming workers) to help him to carry on farming business daily tasks, e.g. picking up friuts, feeding pigs, cows, sheeps to eat food daily. These daily farming jobs are very important to influence this New Zealand farmer's meats or fruits sale number whether they can be easy or diffcult to sell in New Zealand supermarkets , if these farming workers can own encough farming knowledge or skill to know how to pick up fruits method and make judgement to know whether it is right time to pick up the kind of fruits from the trees , as well as know how feed this pigs, sheeps, cows to eat food in order to let they are better health. Consequently, their farming behaviors which can let these animals can provide the best taste and enough meat from these animals to let New Zealander to buy to eat from New Zealand any one supermarket. Even these New Zealand farming workers can know whether the kinds of fruits, e.g. oranges, apples, gapes etc. fruits whether they ought be picked up from the trees at the right time. Consequently, they can make judgement to decide to pick up any kinds of the best taste fruits to let any one New Zealander to buy to eat from any one supermarket in New Zealand. Otherwise, if they do not make judegement to know whether the kind of fruit ought not be picked up because they still need longer time to continue grow up to increase fruit size and better taste from the trees in order to let any one fruit buyer can feel better taste when they eat this kind of fruit later. If they can buy this kind of fruit to eat later, then this New Zealand farmer's his fruit buyers can buy the best taste of this kind of fruit to eat from an yone supermarket in New Zealand. Consequently, many New Zealand supermarkets will choose to buy any kinds of fruits from this farmer fruit supplier when they feel this farmer's fruits can provide more better taste fruits to compare other farmers' fruits.

Thus, due to New Zealand is one farming main income source country. It's any kinds of fruits and meats need to be export to overseas to sell , instead of local sale. It's GDP percent is very high to whole country 's overall income source. So, any one New Zealand farmer individual and any one farming worker individual working behavior will influence its economy whether it is influenced to grow or recession possible. Moreover, it also seems that farming workers' farming knowledge and skill will influence themselves farming daily activities to achieve the aim of the number of increase or decrease to any kinds of fruits whether they are better taste or the number of increase of decrease to any kinds of meats whether they are better taste to supply to any one New Zealand fruit or meat buyers to eat from any one New Zealand supermarket. So, it implies that any one New Zealand farming worker individual farming behavior may influence any kinds of fruits or any kinds of meat taste because they are transported to any one supermarket to sell in New Zealand.

Consequently, if New Zealans had many farmers can teach god farming knowledge and skill to let their any one farming workers know how to decide judgement to decide when it is right time to pick up any kinds of fruits from trees , or how to grow them on soil in order to let they can grow rapidly. Then, many different kinds of fruits can be provided to let any one New Zealanders can eat the best taste of fruits when their fruits are supplied to any one New Zealand supermarkets. Even, if they knew how to feed foods to pigs, cows, sheeps to eat daily. Then they can be more health and they can provide the best taste of meats to let any one New Zealanders can buy their meats from any one New Zealand supermarkets. Moreover, their fruits and meats can be transported to overseas to let any one country fruits or meats buyers can choose any kinds of New Zealand meats and fruits to buy to eat from themselves countries supermarkets. Then, many overseas fruit and meat buyers will perfer to choose New Zealand any kinds of fruits or meats to buy to compare other countries fruits or meats to buy when they go to any one local supermarkets.

On conclusion, it seems that New Zealand farming workers themselves farming behavior may influence their farming employers any kinds of fruits or meats sale number and income because their farming task behaviors must influence whether their fruits or meats taste are the better taste or worse taste to compare their other local farmers (the farmer competitors) whose fruits or meats taste. If tthe farmer's any one farming worker can be trained to learn how to know to feed animals skill and when is the most right time to pick up any kinds of fruits from trees or how to grow them on the soil methods. Due to these farming worker individual farming behavior may influence his different finds of fruits and meats sale number to be increase or decrease, so these any one New Zealand farmer must need to depend on any one farming worker whose farming working methods, if their farming working behaviors can be the best to influence any kinds of fruits to grow rapid or any kinds of pigs, cows, sheeps animals grow up rapidly , then their sale number may be increase significantly and their taste can be improved to let any New Zealand or overseas meat or fruit buyer to buy to eat to feel from any one New Zealand or overseas supermarkets, then New Zealand's agriculture industry must be influenced to increase. In the world, any one fruit or meat buyer must choose to buy New Zealand's fruit and meat to eat in prefer to compare other countries' fruits and meats. So, New Zealand's GDP may be influenced to raise from any one New Zealand farming worker individual farming working behaviors.

www.ingramcontent.com/pod-product-compliance
Ingram Content Group UK Ltd.
Pitfield, Milton Keynes, MK11 3LW, UK
UKHW040031200726
13854UKWH00001B/472

9 798888 495049